KAISHA MCCREA

# Life, Love & Legacy

*Honoring My Father William Lee Holman*

First edition

Editing by Andrea Price
Editing by Maurice Gray, Jr
Cover art by Fred Nash

This book was professionally typeset on Reedsy.
Find out more at reedsy.com

# Contents

# Foreword

This book has been over forty-five years in the making.

I began writing this book by interviewing family, and friends , it was apparent that my father's death left a void in their hearts. My mom shared with me, for the first time, several things about my father, and one story sticks out. She told me that my father would come home and park near the window of our home, and I would go to the window to look for him. He drove a truck and I heard that sound when he arrived. She then told me that after he died, I went to that window every day for a long time. I imagine I kept waiting for him to return and kept looking for him.

This story broke my heart. It made me wonder what emotions filled my little one-and-a-half-year-old mind and heart as I looked for my father, who never returned. Today, as I write this book, I get the opportunity to see my father return to my life through memories shared by his family and his closest remaining friends. I have been given the opportunity to provide closure to that little girl who kept looking for her father every day for a long time. This particular memory of me looking for him symbolizes my gap in remembering my father and growing up without him. Mom was wonderful, but this void remained with me from childhood until now.

I am excited to learn more about who my father, William Lee Holman, was in more extensive detail, from the child, man, father, brother, son, cousin, uncle, friend, and husband. This is a journey to capture my father's memories to share with our family and for myself is one I don't take lightly. I am honored to be able to share his life and legacy with others and have questions answered for myself.

Come and enjoy as I explore the different facets of his life and fond memories shared by family and friends. I hope you enjoy the legacy I share about my father, and my desire is that others will be able to cherish and share memories of loved ones lost so that families can see the power of love following a loss and how to continue to grieve and love at that same time. I hope the power of legacy and living a life well, regardless of your age, comes through, and I hope that the power of love shines through the pages as we discuss the love of a father for his daughter, family, friends, and others and how the power of love and family can turn tragedy into promises and joy out of pain.

This book is dedicated to the family he left behind: his parents, wife, siblings, cousins, other family members, and friends. Today, his remaining siblings are one brother and three sisters. He was the first of the siblings to die, leaving a void that continues today.

This book is also dedicated to the 18-month-old me who is navigating life now, over forty-five years later, with a desire to learn more about my father and his legacy as I continue to live and grow to share with future generations.

Imagine knowing your father died when you were young ,not having a full understanding of his life and impact or any memories of him. Imagine growing up with a void you know exists but not being able to fully pinpoint what was needed to completely fill this void or heal these wounds and fragments in your life.

Well, this is how I felt before I started writing this book on my father. As far as I can recall, I knew my father died when I was very young, but didn't have a good understanding of the impact he had on his family, community, and friends until I began writing this book. I spent time capturing memories of my father, William Lee Holman, from friends and family, and this was the medicine I didn't know my body, heart, and soul needed until I started this process. I was given divine instruction to write this book, and it has left me with so much more peace and understanding. I am a stronger and more complete person today as I was able to receive facts, memories, and stories from friends and family that created a bridge from me to my father. This bridge will help me share his story with my children, other family members, friends, and future generations. It is with this intention that I share my father's life with others to honor his memory and legacy.

I had a few tangible items of his shared with me by mom and several pictures of the two of us. My mom told me that they took a lot of pictures, and these, for a long time, were some of the best memories I had of him. This journey has allowed me to receive so much more of the intangibles that provide a complete view of my father from his childhood to his death. I got a chance to know him as a person from several viewpoints across his life. This was a journey I didn't choose, but it chose me, and I am eternally grateful for the chance to share my father's memories with others. I will continue his legacy and share the love expressed and captured through talks with friends and family in this book as a tribute to my father's life, love, and legacy.

# Chapter 1- Some Bonds Are Forever

**Some bonds are forever:**

*"As long as you speak my name, I will live forever," African Proverb.*

In my family, we care about each other, and our relationships are very important to us. My father, William Lee Holman, died at the age of 26 1/2 in a tragic car accident on Friday, January 21, 1977. He left behind a 26-year-old widow and me, not yet two years old. I would say the need for this book started on that day.

I don't remember the day or the year I realized my father was no longer alive. I don't remember the first person who told me or how old I was when I did. I can only recall all my life knowing my father died in a car accident when I was around two years old, and that's how I lived my life.

*My father and I in front of our home.*

I am the only child of my father and was named by him. He gave me my first, middle, and last names. My middle name is Tena, and means loveable. As I talked with family, I could hear the love he had for me, the love our family had for him, the love shared by my parents and the love he had for family and others. I was too young to recall any memories of my father; all the memories

2

I had of him, as I was growing up, came from seeing pictures of us together. I remember seeing his picture in the bedroom I slept in when I visited my grandparents, his parents. It was on top of the dresser in a frame, and I saw his face whenever I visited them. I don't remember exactly when it happened, but one time I went for a visit, and his picture was no longer there.

**The Journey Begins**

*"He was not an ordinary person. He may have come from an ordinary back-ground, but he worked hard to be an extraordinary person." Aunt Earline McClary (whom I affectionately call Aunt Missy)*

This quote summarizes my father's life and stayed with me during my interviews.

"He was brilliant." King Fogle *(one of his closest friends)*

**A void in the family**

*"His smile was what was most unique about him- felt like he was happy inside and very welcoming when he saw you." Aunt Sue Cobb*

There wasn't much talk about my father as I was growing up – particularly, about his qualities or personality. There was some mention of him but not very often. The people who spoke the most about my father were my grandmother, Eva Holman, my father's mom, and my mom.

Mom mentioned him at times, and we met at least annually in South Carolina with his best friends and their families to continue these connections and bonds. Different family members shared a few facts or memories with me about my father, but nobody I can recall ever really had a longer conversation with me about my father to share more about him. I don't recall anyone really sharing with me the similarities they saw in our personalities or mannerisms, for example. Mom likely did share some similarities with me when I was growing up. I do recall that one time Uncle Lymus, when some family members and I visited him in Nebraska, told me that I had the "same quiet confidence as my father." This was when I was a teenager.

As I write this first chapter, I fight back the tears. The tears because I lost my father, my father who I never got to fully know or have cherished memories

3

to recall. It's hard to remember anything around the age of two. After he died, my mom and I moved back to her hometown of Lake City, SC, from Holly Hill, SC, where we lived, and then my life story had a new chapter. I can't recall how I felt when I left Holly Hill and my grandparents, aunts, uncles, and cousins, but I can only imagine being almost two years old and likely not knowing what was happening. I moved to a new area where another group of aunts, uncles, cousins, and my grandfather lived. This was the extended family I grew up with for the rest of my life while returning for every major holiday and summers to visit my father's side of the family, the Holmans, and reconnect with my grandparents, cousins, aunts, uncles, and church friends.

## Love never dies

*"He was humble and quiet, enjoyed being by himself and interested in education. Doing the best with what he had."* Peter Holman (close 1st cousin of my father)

Let's begin with what I knew about my father's life and what I was given of him before I dreamed of writing this book. I knew he was very smart. Mom shared that he was in Upward Bound, a program for first-generation college students. My father and mother met in college at Claflin College in Orangeburg, SC.

*My father in one of his college yearbooks.*

My grandma shared that he was her "most humble child." I can't remember how old I was when she shared this with me, but I remember when I heard her say that, and the next few weeks or months, I tried to be humble. It didn't always work. I was not really humble. I was the only child, and being the only child, I was familiar with being in the spotlight and having a large amount of attention on me.

My father was the only one of his siblings to attend college directly after high school. He attended college in the early 1970s when several African American students were the first people in their families to attend college. Uncle Joe shared that I sounded like my father when I detailed how I responded to a co-worker to address a concern, during one of our discussions, giving me the impression that he was outspoken.

There are probably other things family members shared with me when I was younger that I don't remember, I ask for forgiveness if I can't recall any key items shared with me when I was that age. Mom told me my father and I share a few physical similarities, like our feet shape and higher hips. I have my father's feet- long, narrow with long toes. My Uncle Odell told me my youngest son, Nathan, looks like my father. He has a very similar physical build to my father - tall, lean and with a similar complexion.

I had the honor to talk to my father's remaining siblings, friends, brothers-in-law, and sisters-in-law to learn more about him. I am thankful to be able to ask my mom about my father, too. I am thankful to my mom for raising me with an open heart and for the support of my family and friends who helped me become who I am today. I thank my extended family, teachers, and stepfather for helping to support and nurture me during my life.

Uncle Odell shared that my father had a "very good, quiet, and humble personality."

### Interviewing Family and Friends

*"He valued different viewpoints. He was a great person, loved people, and a fun person," shared my Mom.*

I started my interviews with family first, then I interviewed friends, classmates, and community friends. The interviewing process took a lot of strength, curiosity, awareness, and patience. I traveled from Virginia to South Carolina to talk with my mom and my father's sisters and brother. One weekend, I spoke to Uncle Odell and Aunt Lula on back-to-back days. I usually took time to decompress and process the information and emotions from the interviews for a few days before I started another interview. I needed time to sit with the stories, new insights, joy, or pain shared.

Everyone that I interviewed was willing and ready to share memories with me. Some were sad at times, but all had many memories to share with me.

I was excited and somewhat nervous when driving to talk with Aunt Lula and Uncle Odell. By the time I met with them, I had a good picture of my father's personality and background but knew they held a special view of him since they were closer in age to each other.

I traveled by myself to interview both Aunt Sue & Uncle Joe and Aunt Lula & Uncle Harold at different times in this process. Around the time I was preparing to travel to visit Aunt Sue and Uncle Joe, a storm passed through the area near, my childhood church I was attending ,that Sunday morning, in New Zion SC. There was even a tornado watch and heavy winds during service before I headed to Columbia, SC to visit and interview them. My discussion with Aunt Sue & Uncle Joe was the first interview I scheduled.

I was determined to start the interview process and didn't change my travels because of the storm moving through the area. As I traveled to my aunt and uncle's house, the rain slowed, and clear skies returned. I felt comfortable with my decision to travel, during the rain, to start this interview and book.

Each interview was unique in that depending on the type of relationship each family member or friend had with my father, the interview's tone could be different, and the type of information shared covered different areas of my father's life and provided additional perspectives.

I arrived at each interview with the same level of curiosity, respect, and gratitude for them taking the time to talk with me and share some sad and joyous memories. I was a bit nervous if I spoke to someone I had not talked to in years or never spoken to before but was able to connect with everyone I spoke with. Each person that I interviewed possessed remarkable memories, and I was astounded by how much information and details they shared with me. I recorded each conversation and was able to capture the key points and themes they shared with me within the pages of this book.

I interviewed the following people to collect their stories and memories to capture in this tribute to my father: my Mom ( Dorothy Fulmore), Susie Cobb, Joseph Cobb, Lula Samuel, Harold Samuel, Odell Holman, Minnie Holman, Olivia Holman, Joseph King, Earline McClary, Earnest Fleming, Levern Fleming, Rodney Holman, Peter Holman, Adam Brown, King Fogle,

Leonard Bodrick, Gerald Mackie, Vernon Williams, and Jerome Clark.

# Chapter 2- Walk a Day in My Shoes

**My Childhood**

*"You had a remarkable father, brilliant, funny, silly, kind-hearted." King Fogle.*

There was a noticeable void in my life while growing up without my father. My Mom did a wonderful job as a single parent, but sometimes, I desired a father figure. When I saw other children with their fathers, it made me sad and was a constant reminder of what I lost and no longer had.

I remember being in ballet classes as a young girl and seeing dads come to pick up their daughters, and once again, this reminded me that I no longer had a father. I recall as a young child having these dreams of him coming back or if maybe there was another sibling out there somewhere that could bring a connection of him back to me also. During those times in the eighties, no one really talked a lot about children who lost a parent or dealing with the death of parents for children. I had no options presented to help me process this reality, loss, and grief. Mom remarried when I was around ten years old and my younger brother, Shawn, was born when I was seventeen years old.

I remember one school picture when I was about three years old, and I looked pretty sad compared to future pictures. I am not really smiling in this picture. It wasn't until recently through attending a session at my church on depression and mental wellness, that I learned that children as young as two or three years old can show signs of depression. I have to wonder what 3-year-old me was feeling and experiencing in that picture. My future school year pictures are happy, and I am smiling. Growing up, I experienced a very good childhood and was a happy, intelligent student, loving and somewhat sensitive child.

*Smiling as I prepare to go to church.*

When visiting some extended family, my grandma would introduce me as William's daughter. As I got older when I met some extended family members on the Holman side, I would introduce myself as William's daughter after sharing my name. Sometimes I would share that I was the granddaughter of Adam and Eva. After saying I was William's daughter, I would usually hear a little statement back from them about something they knew about him or related to his death. Those statements lessened over the years.

My extended family was always kind and happy to meet me, but it was a bit exhausting and somewhat sad for a brief time if his death was mentioned because this reminded me again about the void in my life. I may have felt better if they shared a bit more about his life during those times when I first met someone new in the family. As this was a void that was very present for me. I was able to connect with all my family members which was a trait my mom shared my father was able to do and how he treated everyone well.

**Walking a Day in My Shoes**

*"He really cared about you and loved you. He tried hard to put things in place for a better future for all in the family." Peter Holman*

I remember mom taking me to visit my father's grave in the family burial grounds in Holly Hill, SC every year during my childhood. I believe that continued until I went to college, and our schedules did not align with each other's like when I was a child. I recall we visited on occasions after college, but it was no longer every year. The family burial ground was near one of my aunt's houses, so visiting my father's grave would also include time to visit with my Aunt Margaret. I also enjoyed visiting Aunt Margaret. She had a wealth of information and was always happy to see us.

# Chapter 3 - Reflections From Friends and Family

***The World During the Time My Father Lived ( The Cultural and Political Challenges)***

My father met his college friend Gerald Mackie during their freshman year at Claflin College. He described the world they lived in as such:

*"People still didn't have equal rights, still had a lot of Jim Crow laws in a lot of places. Blacks couldn't go to predominantly White institutions."*

The world was a different place when my father was born in 1950 and during his life until he died in 1977. There were racial and economic disparities, segregation, and discrimination present in our country. As I talked with family and friends, they shared a great perspective of the time for them, the changing landscape of the country, and the fight for equal rights and liberation of black people across the globe, which was a particular focus of my father and several of his friends.

## His Personality

*"Beautiful, calm, mostly quiet, accepting, kind person . He was the kindest person I ever met."* Rodney Holman

*A picture of my father.*

I enjoyed learning more about my father's personality from talking with friends and family. It was great to learn more about him and hear family and friends' different and common responses. This felt like putting together pieces of a puzzle to understand my father better. He had strong beliefs and was opinionated, but he was open and considered different views. I see this as a unique ability.

It is a consensus among family and friends that my father was intelligent. He also wanted to make a difference and improve the lives of others. The family truly loved him.

Mom: " He loved to study. He was accepting of others. He was also very outgoing, and friendly, loved the church, the bible, and his friends, was visionary, and had a lot of plans for the future."

My mom shared that he loved to play games. He was opinionated, according to Uncle Odell. He was an open person, easy for others to talk with.

Some shared he was reserved and quiet, others shared he was funny and outgoing. It depended on his relationship with each person and the different stages in his life that he knew each person. These were some main updates I gathered from talking with friends and family when they shared their memories of his personality.

Cousin Peter, who is four years older than my father, described his person-ality as serious-minded and very determined. He said that when they were growing up together, "He seemed more than a little boy."

Cousin Adam Brown shared that my father's personality was quiet and mild and that he could get along with anybody, even if you didn't know him. He also described him as a jokester. He also told me that my father had the personality to get people to talk and was very engaging and knowledgeable. He described him as kind to people in need and understood the people he would deliver orders to.

Uncle Odell shared my father had a "very good, quiet, and humble personal-ity." Aunt Minnie is married to Uncle Odell, and she remembered my father always smiled and had a big smile. Aunt Minnie asked Uncle Odell if my father was opinionated, to which he replied, "Very opinionated!" We all laughed at that confirmation.

"Intelligent, funny, very intuitive" was how Jerome Clark described my father. He shared that my father "kept him in stitches" and enjoyed being around him. Jerome Clark shared that my father saw him as a little brother, and he, Jerome, helped work for my granddad in farming.

Earline McClary (Aunt Missy): "Outgoing. He had a personality that would draw a person to him. Like he never met a stranger."

Bodrick (met my father while in high school in Orangeburg, SC): "Very affable and open person." Bodrick also shared that my father was "Open and calm, unassuming, almost quiet, very approachable. A true activist. He was a thorough person."

"He was always the leader (in their group involved in activism)." shared Gerald Mackie. "He was an activist at heart. Big champion of social justice and equality." He shared that my father was brilliant and knowledgeable in Black History, and graduated with honors. He described him as "a very approachable person" and always wanted to educate his people about Black History. He shared that at that time in college, Claflin didn't have Black history or African-American Literature courses.

Levern Fleming ( affectionately known as Uncle Bubba): "He was a quiet guy.".

My father was viewed by family and friends through the interviews as cool, calm, and collected, an activist, brilliant, and able to connect to others well.

## Cool, Calm, and Collected was how some described his personality

*"He was a thinker. He was not a mean person. People respected him."* Adam Brown.

Aunt Sue: "He was cool, calm and collected, and like a reserved person."

## His Brilliance was recognized as a part of his personality

*"Brilliant" was the first word my father's close friend King Fogle used to describe his personality when we talked.*

Hearing his friend use the word "brilliant" to begin talking about my father spoke volumes to me and helped me understand the magnitude of his brilliance and the impact he had on those around him and those who knew him best. I was beyond impressed and proud of my father.

## His Ability to connect with Others was recognized as a part of his personality

*"He was committed to what he believed in."* Uncle Joe

*My father most likely talking with Upward Bound students.*

Convictions are important and speak volumes about the type of person my father was. Cousin Rodney also described my father as honest, church-going, and decent.

King Fogle described my father as "Good, kind-hearted, could be funny and mischievous at times- never one to put anyone down. He had an undying love for Black people." King also described him as "shy, mostly with the ladies and a little laid back."

Aunt Lula shared that my father's personality was "outgoing and robust, daring, he would try anything and be friends with anybody." Uncle Harold described him as, "laid-back and courageous."

Cousin Vernon Williams shared that my father's personality was not aggressive and that he liked being around him and shared he had a nice personality and could get along with anyone. He shared that my father liked being precise, was very pleasant, didn't have an aggressive tone when he talked to you, and made you feel comfortable talking with him. "He didn't talk down to people,"he shared. Vernon described my father's voice as a low tone of voice. I would learn more about my father's tone of voice and its similarities to others in the Holman family in an interview with another family member.

Uncle Earnest Fleming: "He was a very concerning, well-rounded, well-versed, caring, and giving person." He shared that he had a personality that people would be connected to and was concerned about his fellow man. He shared that my father was firm but flexible, intelligent, very understanding, well-mannered, very honest, and truthful.

After hearing all these wonderful memories of my father, I was able to connect more pieces of the puzzle of his life, and left me feeling amazed.

## His Activism and Community Involvement

*"He was an activist at heart." Gerald Mackie (college friend)*

Bodrick described my father as a true activist and a thorough person. Bodrick shared that my father would want me to know about his focus on truth and understanding your situation. He shared how my father would pose questions, to be thorough, and was an example of being committed to what you know and how you share that message or information.

He shared my father would want me to know the importance of people like him and the time they experienced during the movement. "It was an interesting time," he added. He shared that everyone in my father's friend group knew about their situation. He shared they were leaders, and my father would want me to value that. I heard more stories and memories of my father's activism in different interviews and this was awesome to hear about in more detail and learn more about this very important aspect of his life.

# Chapter 4- The Interview Process

**Sharing Memories is Powerful**

*"It was a long time ago, but then it wasn't. It's like yesterday in so many ways."*
*Leonard Bodrick*

This statement connected to the essence of this book and being able to talk with my father's family and friends about him. It was over 45 years since my father's death, and in some interviews and our experiences, it was a long time ago, but not so long in many cases based on the amount and details of memories they shared with me. It was like yesterday with the flow of tears and at times cautious pauses in some interviews and different expression of emotions from happiness, joy, and sorrow as we talked about my father. I am thankful that his friends, family, and community members shared these memories.

Some may ask why this book is relevant or needed now. I feel it's because, for many that I interviewed, the void and internal wounds of my father's death are still present. I believe my father had a story and life that needed to be shared, acknowledged, honored, and a legacy to recognize and continue.

I enjoyed talking with my family members about my father's personality and their memories of him. I asked them to go back over 40 years to share what they could remember of his dreams, goals, impact, joys, strengths, struggles, and life. I experienced different emotions when I spoke to different family members.

Cousin Adam's stories made me laugh and were more lighthearted as I enjoyed the stories and memories he shared about the humorous side of my father. Cousin Adam and my father were a few years apart, he was actually my father's nephew and visited during the summers from up North. He shared such fond memories of knowing him and their time during the summers as teenagers. He even shared how my father would tell him to call him "Uncle William" around people he just met in the area and he said he would not call him " Uncle William" but would call him "William". We just laughed at this story. I loved hearing this humorous side of my father's personality.

Cousin Adam's perspective was unique, and I loved hearing every minute. He shared that my father and my Uncle Harold introduced him to Jimi Hendrix music, and he still listens to Jimi Hendrix today. Before talking with Cousin Adam, I didn't know my father liked Rock music. My oldest son, Christian, also likes Rock music. It was fascinating to see how many more pieces of my father's life became clearer for me.

**Sharing my Journey to Interview Friends and Family**

*"Anyone would love to have him as a friend." Aunt Lula*

*My father and cousin Haileab enjoying time together.*

When I started thinking of what I wanted to know about my father during this process I decided to capture the key areas I wanted to learn more about. I realized I wanted to know more about who he was as a person covering his childhood up to death, his personality, hopes, dreams, and challenges. I wanted to hear these stories and learn as much as I could about my father. These are the starting ideas that I discussed with family and friends during our interviews. I decided to ask everyone the same questions to help capture the memories easier and allow for more depth of memories on similar topics. I would change the questions slightly when I met with his friends or in-laws.

I wanted to know more about:

His childhood, His best qualities

His most challenging qualities

His joys, His pain

His successes, His challenges

His legacy, His hobbies

His favorite sayings

His favorite food, His favorite music

His dreams and goals

His heart, His best friends

School memories

Could he sing? Could he dance?

His heart's desire

Who he most reminded you of?

I also wanted to learn anything else they thought he would want me to know about him that I didn't ask about and gave them time to share any additional information they desired during each interview.

## Starting to capture memories shared by family and friends

*"He would want you to know everything about him. He was a just guy." Uncle Harold Samuel.*

As I prepared to begin the interviews with family and friends, I prayed to God that I would just "be" and receive any information shared with me about my father during this time. I was prepared to receive any updates without judgment. I was open to what I might learn about my father and anything shared. I was in for such a beautiful journey, one I could have never imagined.

I started interviewing family about my father in March 2023 and started my interviews with my Aunt Sue and Uncle Joe. Aunt Sue is five years older than my father and shared great memories with me of her younger brother. After Aunt Sue spoke, Uncle Joe shared his memories with me for most of the questions. He agreed with her responses for some questions and had nothing else to add, and sometimes he would add extra facts and information. There were a few times when I could feel that either Aunt Sue or Uncle Joe wanted to share more but couldn't bring themselves to continue to share.

I prepared myself with tissues because I cry easily when talking about some things related to my father, but no tears fell during our discussion. A few times, my eyes widened, and I placed my arms on my knees and slowly rocked back and forth slightly. When we started talking and going through the questions I provided to Aunt Sue in advance, it was difficult for us at times, and it was possibly more difficult for Aunt Sue. The questions I asked required my aunt and uncle to go back over 40 years to recall. That would be a challenge for anyone.

After the first few questions, we became more at ease, and a few responses made us laugh. It was a good discussion, and we focused more on my father's life and not very much on his death, though they did share updates with me about his tragic accident.

After our discussion, I thanked my aunt and uncle and acknowledged this took a lot for them. I am thankful they shared the memories they recalled for the questions I asked, and other memories they had. These were precious to me. Aunt Sue also recommended I talk with one of their nephews, Adam Brown, who was close to my father as they grew up.

One reason I may not have cried during my discussion with my aunt and uncle was that I cried on the way over to their house, and I prayed and asked God for strength and to allow me to "be" in the moment of this discussion with them and to help me receive anything shared.

I left my Aunt Sue and Uncle Joe's house, drove a street over, and shared with my Aunt Lula that I was writing a book about memories of my father and would like to ask her some questions in the coming months. She was happy to hear this update and shared that she thought this was a good idea and brought back memories of her brother.

I brought my father's senior year high school yearbook from 1970 for my aunts and uncles to see. This brought back memories. They could see my father in several pictures and other people and teachers they remembered. Aunt Lula saw herself in some of the pictures also. It was a beautiful day.

*My father wrote "Power" above most of his pictures in his 1970 Roberts High school yearbook. He is also in the center of lower right picture.*

Aunt Lula Samuel: "He was faithful and obedient to his family, loyal to his community and family members. He made a difference. He was a go-getter."

I interviewed my mom, at her house. We sat on the living room couch and talked. I knew our interview may be the most delicate discussion of them all. Mom and I had a great discussion. I provided questions to her in advance, and I could sense this was a difficult discussion for her and one she likely would prefer to delay or not have. At first, she shared that she may not be able to remember very much based on the number of years that had passed. After our initial questions, mom became comfortable sharing responses to the questions and sharing more details with me. She shared that she tried to block out all of the memories because it was too painful since my father died so suddenly and tragically. At the end of our discussion, I thanked my mom for sharing with me as it would help me learn more about my father, close my gaps, and help my children know more about their grandfather.

One of the most touching memories mom shared with me was about me at the window looking for my father to pull up in his truck after he was gone. She told my Aunt Missy that was such a sad thing. That statement alone shed so much light on my connection with my father at 1 1/2 years old, and I can only imagine how sad and confusing that must have been for me – looking for my father to return, and he never did. That touched my heart so much. I was proud of my mom for being willing to return to a time to share what she could remember with me about my father. I loved everything I was hearing and it's wonderful to see the connections between the interviews with my Aunt and Uncle and then with my Mom. It was a wonderful feeling to start to learn more about my father in a more complete way.

Mom reminded me that we have pictures of us together and how much he loved me. Now I am starting to see the connections and learn more about who my father, William Lee Holman, was as a person, father, husband, sibling, friend, uncle, and more! I am thankful to be able to learn more about him. I am thankful God led me on this journey.

I called my Uncle Odell, who lived in South Carolina, to check in on him as he was ill, and I typically would call to check in on him to see how he was doing. On this particular day, I shared that I was writing a book collecting memories of my father and would like to interview him in person this summer. He was happy to do this. Sharing this would give him purpose and something to look forward to. We met for an interview during the summer, and Uncle Odell passed away about three months later that fall. I am thankful to have met with him and include his words, thoughts, and memories of my father, his older brother, in this book.

My journey to interview family and friends lasted about six months, and most of the interviews were over the phone, but I met with most of my father's siblings and my mom in person. During the interviews, I met a person who attended high school with my father, Evangelist Joseph King. That was such a surprise. He was introduced to me by my cousin Jemal Cobb. I shared his insights in the book also. It was amazing to know that someone that attended high school with my father had such a great memory of him. I believe they were a couple of years apart in high school. His brother and my father both attended Upward Bound together.

**Emotions are good**

*"He was a jewel." Aunt Lula*

This statement was so true and present throughout my interviews as I heard more and more about the uniqueness of my father from his personality, intellect, impact, love, and commitment to his beliefs, family, friends, and community.

There is a line in the song, "My Testimony," by Bishop Marvin Sapp, a Christian minister and singer, that says," So if you see me cry, it's just a sign that I'm alive." I am a singer and love music and ministering music at church. Today during church service, after singing with the church band, I observed someone hugging their father-in-law, and I was overtaken by emotion. The emotions came suddenly and surprised me.

My friend and writing coach reminded me that as I write this book with my 'head,' in terms of planning & activities that I should remember to include my heart and feelings. I remember sharing with her that I would. Before I saw this moving image of the love shown with a simple act of a hug, I prayed to God that

I would share my feelings in this book, and suddenly a few minutes later, as the musicians were singing and playing a beautiful song that the tears began to flow. I realized I cried for the void that I experienced with losing my father and not having a father to embrace, similar to the hug I saw. I also understand that there is something as precious and priceless as a bond between a daughter and father or father-in-law. My heart was touched, and the tears came.

*My father and I at home.*

# Chapter 5- Friendship and Lasting Memories

**Friends of My Father**

*"If you couldn't get along with Brother William, something's wrong."* Uncle Earnest Fleming

I am thankful that my mom stayed in contact with my father's friends from college. We would gather with their friends in SC for dinner and fellowship every year. I started going with my mom to these gatherings at an early age- I can't remember how old and up until I was in high school or college. I remember attending one gathering after I graduated from college. That was the last gathering I recall attending as I moved to Delaware a few years after graduating from college.

I remember visiting one of their friends, Clarence Burke, nicknamed Burke, and his wife, Gladys, in Washington DC, or northern VA, when I was little. I remember the fun I had visiting them and the time they spent with me. I can recall recording a cassette tape singing a song from Diana Ross during one of the visits to their house. They didn't have any children then, so I received a lot of attention from them. Years later, they became parents of five children, and my time around them dwindled.

Some of my father's closest college friends were General Thomas, Burke, and King Fogle. The friend gatherings were often held at General's house in South Carolina. Burke and General passed away a few years ago but I was able to know them, and they attended my wedding. I have a picture with the four of us at my wedding. My mom still has this picture on her fireplace mantel today.

I had the honor to interview one of my father's best friends, King Fogle, the last surviving friend of his inner circle. We had a great time talking about his memories of my father. I could hear the pure joy and strong friendship, and I was amazed at how much he remembered and the specific details he shared. I asked him to share memories about my father from more than 40 years ago; he still could remember when they first met in 1968 and their time spent in Upward Bound. I was beyond impressed. I could hear the joy of their friendship through the phone as we talked. It was so cool to learn that they were roommates in college for three years, which is awesome. I never had the same roommate for over a year, so I knew they were close. I enjoyed learning more about my father during these years of his life from his friend, King. I learned more about his late teenage and early adult years, which was a new insight.

I learned that he liked sports, especially baseball. I also learned that my father and King were both accepted into graduate school at Atlanta University, but they had to return home due to the cost of college and not receiving financial aid or housing. This was so eye-opening for me. The first word his friend used to describe my father was "brilliant." It was amazing to hear what his friend expected him to become if his life had not ended so early.

It is amazing to see the love, bond, and impact of friendship that remains after death. I am happy to see that he had such great friends and to hear how close they were. King also added a layer of insight to the culture and events in our country during the time they met in 1968. It was a few months after Dr. Martin Luther King Jr's assassination and in the middle of various waves of student activism, protests, and the Black Power Movement. It helped further set the stage for me to understand the world they lived in at that time. This time period was a time of promise, unrest, and uncertainty.

## Honoring the Dead

*"He was a good man, a loyal person. He loved you, he loved his wife, loved his family, loved his community." Aunt Olivia*

I interviewed Aunt Olivia, and it was great talking with her. She was my first interview over the phone instead of in person. When I told her that I was writing a book on memories of my father and asked if she could share in the place of Uncle Lymus, who died two years ago, she said yes. I provided questions to Aunt Olivia in advance, similar to the ones shared with Aunt Sue.

Aunt Olivia had very clear memories to share with me. She told me that after my father's death, she and Uncle Lymus arrived home from Germany to see us, and that I thought Uncle Lymus was my father, based on how much they resembled each other. She shared she could tell my father spent a lot of time with me. She shared how much he loved me and mom and what a good, kind, and loving person he was. She mentioned his intelligence and ability to debate on any topic. She felt that had he lived longer, he would have gone far and could have been a politician.

Peter Holman (cousin): "He really cared about you and loved you. He tried hard to put things in place for a better future for all in the family."

I asked family and friends several questions during our interviews, and one of these questions was:

### What would he want me to know about him?

The main items they shared they felt my father would want me to know were related to his love for me and his family, his obedience and impact, his views, and his legacy.

*"He would really be proud of what you're doing. He really loved his wife as well. He loved his family. He would be pleased about what you're doing, putting his memories in a written document to share with your children."* Gerald Mackie

Some quotes that convey his love for me and the time he spent with me are:

"How much he loved you and how much time he spent with you. He seemed to always have you." Aunt Sue

"He was a very lovable and honorable person and accepted people as they were. He would want you to do the same." Rodney Holman

Uncle Earnest expressed that my father loved me and his family. He shared that he " wanted the best for you and would want you to continue to build that legacy." He also said, "Always maintain where you are going in life. It's not about how you start but how you finish. He was that type of person."

**His obedience and Impact:**

"He was faithful and obedient to his family, loyal to his community and family members. He made a difference. He was a go-getter." Aunt Lula Samuel

**His beliefs and views:**

"Failure was not an option for him." Aunt Missy

"How he cared, what he tried to achieve."Cousin Vernon Williams

*A picture from his 1970 Roberts High Yearbook. My father is standing in the center of the picture.*

# Chapter 6 - A Powerful Legacy

**The Power of Legacy**

*"Best analytical mind, analyzed political concepts and issues with clarity and could take a position ( political analysis). Great debater." King Fogle*

"Power" is the name my father wrote over several of his pictures in his high school yearbook. I learned when I flipped through his yearbook that he was the editor of the yearbook. I was also the editor of my high school yearbook and on the yearbook staff one year in college. I was also the editor of the newsletter in high school.

His friend King shared that my father was called the name "Power" by another student in college, and that person called King "Glory" also. He shared that this person would say here comes the "Power and the Glory" based on their activism when he saw them.

"He would be proud of you. You have that drive to work hard, set goals, and reach them. That's the kind of person he was. Hard work does pay off. You have to work hard to preserve and have that grit to stick with it. Reach your fullest potential and stand out." Aunt Earline McClary

**I asked family and friends to share what my father was known for:**

We each have an opportunity to have an impact and leave our mark on the world, community or families and make a difference. I learned from talking with family and friends that he was a great debater and very intelligent. Aunt Olivia shared that my father could debate on any subject.

*He was known for being a Leader*

*"Social justice activist to his heart. He ate, slept, and breathed activism in any aspect."* Gerald Mackie.

He was viewed as a leader and had many great qualities shared by friends and family. He was also a person that was friendly.

### He was known for standing up for justice

*"Standing up for justice, he was a righteous person, wanting everything to be done right."* Aunt Sue

I learned more about my father's level of activism and commitment to equal rights and liberation for Black people during my interviews. I was impressed by the impact he had and the work he was involved with during his life.

Bodrick said that in college, my father was known as "one of those radical guys on campus", but that my father and his friends were "**smart**, radical guys." We both laughed at this distinction because we both agreed there's a difference between the two.

He had Pan-African views, according to my Uncle Joe, and he shared with me that the two of them agreed not to discuss their political differences around family. Uncle Joe supported the Republic of New Afrika's views at that time. "It was a time," Aunt Sue said.

"He was truly an activist, knew Black history, which was rare in the South at that time. He would fight for whatever he believed in and didn't mind ruffling feathers. He was not afraid." Gerald Mackie

### He was known for his intelligence

*"Very smart, had to have the last word when arguing with each other."* Uncle Harold

Aunt Lula shared he was known for his intelligence and that he spoke with understanding and confidence. His intelligence and understanding were very present at church also. Aunt Lula shared that some people would call him Mr. Professor in the church. She shared he was awesome at explaining the word of God to people and was the Sunday School Superintendent.

Cousin Vernon: "His intelligence and wit" was what he was known for.

### He was known for debating

Cousin Vernon shared how my father was part of a debate team in college and that this was "a big thing". He recalled his mom, Aunt Margaret, saving paper clips of the newspaper article that featured the Claflin College World Bowl team in the Orangeburg Times and Democrat and that people were talking about their team in the area.

Being a great debater and knowledgeable about politics were some of my father's strengths shared by King Fogle.

### He was known for his personality

*"He was a very warm, receptive, friendly person, kind-hearted, generous, anybody could get along with him." Uncle Earnest Fleming*

I learned so much about my father's personality and how he treated others. It was great to hear and learn more about the wonderful person he was.

### Not honoring the dead is a disservice to them and those left behind

*"He was a gem," shared Aunt Lula.*

It is such a disservice to our loved ones when we don't honor their memories after they die. They have left a legacy and made an impact. Others should remember their efforts and love. It's a disservice to those left behind who didn't get a chance to know them or those too young, like me when a loved one dies. It helps us close gaps we have about ourselves, our personality, and history and can help direct or influence choices we make or don't make. It allows us to see ourselves as complete and not broken, strong and not weak, enough and not in lack, powerful and not different, unique and valued.

Our history and legacy are shaped and formed by those before us, and we must share their lives with those who remain to help each other grow, flourish, and shine through the loss of loved ones, particularly the loss of a parent or close family member.

We want to honor the dead to show our love and remember the joy, sorrows, and fun we had with them. It's okay to remember them in similar ways to how we remember older loved ones who passed away. We can talk about them with joy and good memories and smile, laugh, and, when needed, shed a tear. It's okay. It shows how much we cared for, loved and missed them. Let's take time to share memories of those we lost with the family that remains to help continue their legacy and provide strength, connections, wisdom, and love, in particular, to children whose parents died or close family members.

SCIENCE CLUB

Advisor: Mrs. W. M. Thomas

*In this picture, my father wrote "Holman" above himself. This really made it easy to locate him in his Roberts High School 1970 yearbook.*

# Chapter 7- Family Bonds and My Father's Key Strengths

**Sharing Memories is Powerful**

*"Very kind and caring person and loved everybody; wasn't hard to get along with. Treated others like he would treat his family. He had a loving spirit" is how Uncle Odell shared that my father wanted to be remembered.*

I shared with Cousin Adam during our interview that Uncle Odell shared with his daughter Lindsey that my oldest son, Nathan, looks a lot like my father. After we talked, I shared a picture of Nathan, along with myself and my oldest son, Christian, with Cousin Adam in an email. He agreed that Nathan looked just like his grandfather.

I could see the resemblance over time after family shared this with me and when I compared younger pictures of my father from high school or college with Nathan, especially high school pictures. I shared a few pictures of my father with my oldest son, Christian, and asked if anyone looked like him in the family. This has been a great opportunity to connect my children with more extensions of our family on my father's side. They were able to meet my father through the memories of family and friends and include his legacy in their lives. I am honored to be able to be a link to help share these memories with my children and help fill in the many gaps I had regarding my father. My life feels more complete as I learn more about myself and my father.

MEMBERS: W. Holman, V. Gaines, J. Asbury, M. White, Y. Clark, J. Ra
King, Advisor -- Mrs. W. M. Spells.

*Picture of my father (1st student on lawn from the left) with the Upward Bound
group from 1970 Roberts High School yearbook.*

It was no coincidence that I had a few cousins who shared different facts about
my father over the years with me. Their updates helped me stay connected to
my father's memory.

Cousin Kojo shared that his mom, Aunt Sue, and her remaining siblings in
pictures would often line up by birth order and left a space for my father. That
was shocking and special to hear. My cousin Jemal shared a couple of years ago
when he arranged for my father and our grandparents' graves to be cleaned.
He shared a picture before their grave sites were cleaned, and after they were
cleaned, and shared a closer picture of my father's grave and headstone with
me. I have enclosed a picture of his headstone below.

*My father's grave and headstone.*

Cousin Jemal also shared a few additional updates connected to my father with his sister Dara who shared with me. One of these updates was a picture of my father in his daishiki and another was when his daughter met a professor at

Claflin University who knew my father.

The final connection I made before writing this book was meeting a Gullah tour guide in Hilton Head, SC in December 2022. When I shared that my parents graduated from Claflin after he shared he attended Claflin. I shared with him my father was William Holman and he told me that he remembered my father. That was a shock and a final confirmation that I was doing what I was supposed to do. I shared with my mom my discussion with the Gullah tour guide, and she was able to find him in one of her Claflin College yearbooks and texted his picture to me to confirm the person. This felt like a divine reminder to begin writing this book because what are the chances I would meet someone in Hilton Head, SC, who attended college with my father in the 1970s?

## Family

*"He was a people person, and had kindness for people, especially relatives."* Adam Brown

My father, I learned through my interviews, shared a close bond with his family and was very protective. My aunts, uncles, and friends shared how much he loved my mom and me and his extended family. He took care of me well and was a good father and caring. He read to me before I was born. The family truly loved him. I remember my mom sharing that he didn't use "baby talk" to speak to me but used regular language with me instead.

When I talked with Cousin Vernon Williams, he shared he had "so many memories." I think that captures the essence of my time talking with friends and family, that they had so many memories of my father. It was amazing to hear the stories they shared from over 40-60 years ago. These stories are a testament that love truly never dies.

My father was a good brother to his siblings. He had older siblings, two are still alive, and two younger siblings who are alive. His youngest sibling, Cousin Rodney, later moved in with my father and mother after they graduated from college and returned to my father's hometown of Holly Hill, SC.

Aunt Sue shared he was a good little brother and obedient son.

Aunt Olivia shared he had a great relationship with Uncle Lymus, and his brother gave him his 1971 Green Torino. I never heard about this car until Aunt

Olivia shared this story.

Interviewing people who knew my father was truly a beautiful and wonderful experience. A few tears were shed during discussions, along with some laughter. In one interview, we listened to an old song from the 1970s. The song was "It's Been a Long Time" by The New Birth. It was a unique experience to hear the love, memories and sometimes feel the pain and sorrow shared in our discussions. I was thankful for the opportunity to speak to each person who shared stories and memories they had so many years ago. A clear message to me was the love , friendship and admiration they shared for and with my father .

Some family members I interviewed lived in the same town as my father, some lived outside of Holly Hill, and one would visit during the summers. Some family members on my mother's side met him after they were engaged or married. It was an amazing and eye-opening experience to hear from each of them. I am in awe of how much everyone remembered about my father and the memories they kept and shared. He was described as very obedient and a hard worker.

"He loved his parents very much and was a good son." Peter Holman

Cousin Peter shared that my father was a great cousin and sociable. When I interviewed Cousin Adam Brown, he shared a perspective of my father in his teenage years, his sense of humor, and how close they were. The two of them were very close and similar in age. Adam was my father's nephew and visited when he was 14-17. Though he was his nephew, they were more like brothers.

My father, Adam, and Uncle Odell would share a bed when he visited. He shared they talked a lot and daydreamed. This was an interesting view of my father as a teenager. He shared that my father taught him manners and how to talk to adults regardless of race by saying, "Yes Sir or Yes Ma'am."

My father helped my grandfather with his farming business. When his older brother Lymus moved to Boston, he took on additional responsibility with the workers and the work. I could hear in some of the interviews the distinction of some calling him "William Lee" instead of just by his first name, "William." Aunt Minnie told me that she recalled there was another William Holman in Holly Hill, which may be why a lot of people called my father "William Lee."

One of the most touching interviews I experienced was with my cousin Rodney. He lived with my parents when my father returned to Holly Hill after college from 1974 until my father died in 1977. My heart ached for him as he shared memories of my father with me. I could hear the love and pain of his loss so present today. As I prepared to write his memories, I had to pause to wipe tears from my eyes. What a loving testament to the bond they shared and the difference my father and mother made in his life.

"William Lee was my heart and soul, and so was your mom," Cousin Rodney said. My father took Rodney everywhere, and he traveled many times in the same truck that my father had his accident. He shared memories of their experiences and the time my father took with him. He shared my father taught him how to chop wood and took him on his first college trip to visit Claflin College. He told me that my father treated him like a miniature adult, and he really appreciated that. Following my father's death, Cousin Rodney said his life was not the same. He later moved to New York to rejoin his mother and father after high school graduation. He felt his life would have turned out much better had my father lived longer and he could continue to stay with us. My father's death was the greatest pain he experienced until he experienced the death of one of his children.

My father and Aunt Lula were two years apart, with my father being older than her. Aunt Lula and my father grew up together, and I didn't realize how close in age they were until I started working on this book and saw them in the same 1970 high school yearbook together. It was a joy to hear the stories Uncle Harold and Aunt Lula shared of their times growing up with my father. My father would watch after Aunt Lula and Uncle Odell, who was four years younger than my father when my grandparents went to work. Both Aunt Lula and Uncle Odell described him as protective. Aunt Lula shared he was "very protective" of them. Uncle Harold shared great memories of the two of them being friends and growing up through childhood and adolescent years together. I had no idea Uncle Harold and my father were close friends until I started writing this book. My father and Uncle Harold were one year apart, with Uncle Harold being the oldest. They had known each other since 1959 or 1960 and attended church together.

"I loved my brother." Aunt Lula. She shared he was always a humble and normal guy, like everyone else growing up.

*Picture from left to right of Grandma ( Eva Holman), Uncle Odell, Aunt Lula, Cousin Rodney and my father.*

## The Power of Love

*"Seems like we didn't have enough time to be with him."* Uncle Odell

Talking with Uncle Odell and Aunt Minnie showed the strong love my uncle had for his older brother and the present grief he still experienced. In our discussion, we could laugh and shed a few tears while we shared. It was a very delicate discussion but necessary for collecting memories of my father from his younger brother. Uncle Odell shared that my father was a "good-mannered young man and respected everybody." Uncle Odell shared they lost some years together when my father attended college. He shared that my father taught him a lot and that he loved his brother. Aunt Minnie asked my Uncle to share the nickname my father gave him.

I never knew Uncle Odell had a nickname or that my father had a nickname. Uncle Odell shared that my father would call him "Fox" and "Redd Fox". I asked him why he called him that. He answered because he was "red," which meant his skin was lighter. Aunt Minnie, Uncle Odell, and I just burst out in laughter. That was so funny and unexpected. This was another example of my father's sense of humor. Uncle Odell also shared that my father had a nickname, "Day." He couldn't remember why he was called this name. That was cool to find out that my father had a nickname, and this was the first time that I heard of this name.

Uncle Odell shared that my father protected his younger siblings and me. My father made a good impression on my mom's family before they got married. He had a good relationship with his in-laws and was close with them. I enjoyed interviewing my Aunt Missy, Uncle Earnest and Uncle Levern (Bubba) to share their memories of him. It was an eye-opening experience to see the connections and friendship they had with my father, too. Aunt Missy shared how she and my father competed with each other with vocabulary and tried to challenge each other.

Aunt Missy: "In speaking, he didn't want to use ordinary words but higher level words." She remembers him studying Reader's Digest, and they were friends.

Aunt Missy told me that "He was a leader." In her opinion, the family depended on him for several things. He, my mom, and I lived behind my grandparents' house in our mobile home in Holly Hill. We were within walking distance from my grandparents. Aunt Missy told me that my mom shared that in college, my father was very competitive, loved to debate social issues, and enjoyed social justice. Aunt Missy was a few years older than my parents and also attended Claflin College.

Cousin Vernon shared my father was a "true friend."

"He always looked up to granddaddy, respected his father regardless of his dad's limitations, and loved his family," shared Cousin Vernon. He told me how my father helped my grandfather with his business and shared an example of how he suggested and ran the process of creating a stockpile approach when hauling wood for customers. He shared my father was "always trying to improve, to do better."

Uncle Earnest shared that my father and mother visited him and Uncle Abraham (his brother, now deceased) at Jackson State University and how much it meant for them to see family from South Carolina visiting them in Jackson, Mississippi—"we were very surprised." Uncle Earnest shared he met my father after he married my mom in 1974 since he and Uncle Abraham were out of state attending college when my parents got married. He described my father as a very devoted father and very respectful to his family and his in-laws. He shared my father was a provider and worked hard for his family. He saw him as very family-oriented. " He worked hard for you and your mom, that I know," he shared.

"He was a good man," Uncle Bubba shared. My uncle said that my father took care of me very well, that he wouldn't let me cry, and that he walked with me at night. Uncle Bubba visited my parents a couple of times when they lived in Holly Hill, and later moved in with me and my mom in Holly Hill after my father's death until we moved to Lake City, SC.

## My Father had many Strengths

One of the questions I asked during the interviews was about my father's key strengths. I wanted to understand what he was really good at and understand these better. These were some of my father's strengths shared during our discussion. I was happy to hear all the wonderful strengths my father possessed and shared with others.

## His Determination

My father was a very determined person. Cousin Peter shared that he seemed to have some power and strength, which he described as determination.

## His mind and ability to respond quickly to others

"The ability to think was his strength," shared Uncle Odell.

Uncle Odell described my father as the "thinker of the family and very intelligent." I heard so many ways his intelligence was admired and recognized by others when I spoke with friends and family. He had a unique ability to communicate with others effectively and with knowledge.

"He was able to respond to people quickly when people had different questions and was able to stand up and defend himself." Aunt Sue

Uncle Harold shared that my father was good at math. He said my grandfather asked my father to run a store out of the bus where they sold drinks out of a tub instead of working in the fields. The bus was used to transport or carry the field hands (workers), and my father drove the bus. This showed how strong my father's math skills were to be asked to run the store for my grandfather. Uncle Harold believed my father was a teenager at that time.

"His mind, intelligence, ability to make people laugh." Jerome Clark

### Kept his commitments- Dependable and Reliable

*"If he said he would do something, he would always do it for you and never procrastinate. He was always there for you." Aunt Lula*

He could be counted on and kept his commitment and word to others is what I learned from some of the interviews with family. Uncle Earnest shared that my father would stay with tasks he started until he finished them. "He would follow through. You could count on him."

### His confidence inspired others

*"How much confidence he had in himself. He compared himself with anyone else, Black and White. It didn't matter. He was just as good," said Cousin Vernon.*

"You just as good," my father would say to Cousin Vernon. My father's confidence directly impacted Cousin Vernon as he recalled how my father's view of himself helped him. Cousin Vernon shared that my father's confidence extended to how he viewed his dark complexion also, during a time when some did not view dark complexion in our African American community as positive and children, he recalled, were bullied for their darker complexion.

He looked up to my father because both were of a dark complexion, and shared my father's complexion "didn't bother him at all, and he carried himself with dignity." He recalled my father saying how he viewed himself to be just as good when compared to others.

"I'm just as good as him. It ( race, color) doesn't matter. " Cousin Vernon recalls my father shared.

During the interviews, I wanted to understand who today or previously reminded family and friends of my father. This is part of his legacy and continued connection with us.

The question I asked was:

**Who did my father remind you of in the family ?**

*"He's kind of unique," said Cousin Vernon of my father.*

I added this question during the interviews after my initial interviews. I often heard the similarities he shared with my grandfather or grandmother. One of the unique responses I heard was that my father's voice was similar to my grandmother's, his mom's, by Uncle Harold.

Uncle Harold shared that all the Holmans mainly had softer voices, including my grandfather. This was interesting for me to hear since I am sometimes asked about the softness of my voice, and now I can see most of my Holman family have the same type of voice. Some shared he resembled my grand-mother.

The similarities shared by some that he had with my grandfather were his ability to provide for his family, his helping spirit, his knowledge of scripture and religion, his good work ethic, business sense and his faith.

"He made sure to always have food for his family like his father," said Aunt Lula. She added, "He would pray to God before starting a task, too, like his father. He was always helping people, similar to his father" she added.

Aunt Lula shared that my father reminded her of Cousin Adam Brown, their nephew, and their cousin Allen Dennis growing up. Aunt Minnie shared that he resembled his mother. He was described to have warmth similar to my grandmother by Jerome Clark.

# Chapter 8- My Father's Childhood to Adulthood

**His Childhood**

*"He had chores to do – pears, peaches. He was a good and hard worker," shared Uncle Odell.*

My father was the middle child and third born to my grandparents, Eva and Adam Holman, in Holly Hill, SC. He was five years younger than my Aunt Sue. She recalled he loved to follow her around. It amazed me that Aunt Sue could recall the fondest memory she had of him, which involved her falling out of a tree. He was trying to join her in the tree, and she reached down to pull him up into the tree, fell, and broke her arm. He had four older siblings from granddad's first marriage, Eva Lee, Margaret, George, and Vernell. When my father was growing up, he worked and watched his younger siblings when his parents went to work after the older siblings left home. He was described as protective by both Uncle Odell and Aunt Lula.

*From left to right ( My father, Uncle Odell and Aunt Lula) as young children.*

My grandfather managed workers for several farms in Holly Hill, and my grandma was his bookkeeper.

Aunt Minnie remembered seeing Uncle Odell with my father in the fields, and that my father, as the older brother, taught Uncle Odell what to do. My father continued to do farm work for his father in the summers when he was in college.

## Teenage Years

*"We were too busy working to play sports."* Cousin Adam Brown

Cousin Adam Brown and my father shared a close bond as nephew and uncle but were more like brothers. I learned who some of his closest friends were, including family members and neighborhood or community people and adults, as he got older and returned home from college. Cousin Adam recalled that Uncle Harold and Richard Sweatman were two of my father's closest friends. Richard was one of my father's cousins.

"You can tell when somebody likes you and when somebody loves you." Cousin Adam Brown

*A picture of my father likely as a teenager.*

He was very active in high school, and Aunt Minnie recalled seeing my father in many pictures in one of her brother's yearbooks. He was "known by a lot of people," Aunt Minnie said.

He was an honor student in high school. I was surprised to be able to speak with someone who attended high school with my father. My cousin Jemal shared that there was an evangelist, Robert King, who knew my father well.

He and my father attended Roberts High School together. His brother James Edward King was in the Upward Bound program with my father. He also shared that he and my father had some classes together. He described my father as quiet, non-violent, and interested in Black History and Black Power. He recalled that my father wore daishikis. Evangelist King shared that some remaining members of my father's high school class were still in the area, which was fascinating to hear.

I was impressed when I looked at my father's senior yearbook for 1970 from Roberts High School. I noticed he was the yearbook editor, and voted Most Studious along with other recognitions, such as participating in Upward Bound. Seeing these accomplishments and the areas we have in common was very affirming and inspiring. These were great for me to learn and see. We also both enjoyed Social Studies and Black History.

> This year the staff and I worked hard and diligently to make this annual a success. By dedicating this annual to the war victims from Roberts, we have tried to reflect the feeling of the whole United States of America.
> As we all can see, this country is greatly involved in a moral "conflict of interest" which has reached into Roberts and has taken the cream of the crop. Both graduates and drop-outs. Two of our fine young men have been killed in this cruel war in Viet Nam. We truly look up to these young men as heroes -- heroes to a cause not of their own choosing. We sincerely hope that our comrades have not died in vain -- that the United States will do something honorable about the war. Win it! Lose it! Or Leave It!
> "I would like to express my thanks to our advisors and to all of the staff members who helped to make this annual a success."
>                                    Sincerely yours,
>
>                                    *William Holman*
>
>                                    William Holman
>                                    Editor
>
>                                    103

*My father's words as the Editor of his high school yearbook.*

## College Years

*"God had a plan for his life," said Aunt Lula.*

My father was the first child in his immediate family to attend college. He and his friends were into politics and the movement. Uncle Harold stated that my father was the "designated one" in the family. I took this to mean there were a lot of high hopes placed on him based on his intelligence and desired future.

My father was in a group of four very close friends at college including him, King Fogle, Clarence Burke, and General Thomas. King Fogle is the only remaining member of the circle, and I enjoyed speaking with him. He shared wonderful memories of my father and the experiences they shared, as well as memories of their group. He and King were roommates for three years.

My father had other friends in college, including Gerald Mackie, W. Leggette, and younger students who visited them on campus, including Bodrick and Charles.

Uncle Joe met my father for the first time in 1969 in Washington DC. Aunt Sue and Uncle Joe helped my father financially to complete his junior and senior years in college. Uncle Joe shared he was a bus driver in Boston at that time, and the salary during that time was higher than most salaries. He said that the ability to help my father helped him to become less tight with his money.

"We became fast friends," said King Fogle. King shared that my father was their political theorist. They became close friends based on their intellectual interests. They met each other in June 1968 at Upward Bound and took their first classes together in 1970.

He shared many stories with me of how my father volunteered to be his campaign manager when he ran for an office in college. King lost this campaign. He shared memories of their activism for Black liberation during their years at Claflin College along with Clarence Burke and General Thomas. King shared some of the conferences they attended in support of the total liberation of Black people around the world.

These four friends were scholars and proudly formed the Independent Scholar team that represented Claflin College in the World Bowl and won this academic challenge championship for three years. Their group's pictures and a story of their team were published in 1972 and 1974 in the Orangeburg *Times and Democrat* newspaper. I enclosed a picture from the 1974 newspaper below.

*World Bowl Winners – Advisor, Dr. Douglas Johnson, Clarence Burke, my father, King Fogle and General Thomas ( from left to right).*

The World Bowl was a great accomplishment for my father and his friends. Bodrick shared that the whole group of my father's friends was unassuming and approachable. They involved younger students in their group and they called themselves a Cadre.

The College World Bowl "was very prestigious at that time," shared Bodrick. He described my father, King Fogle, Clarence Burke, and General Thomas as Big Men on Campus (BMOC)after their wins.

King shared how their team was formed and the unique strengths each of them brought to the team. Rocky (Clarence Burke) was a math genius, General had a photographic memory, General and my father knew current affairs and history, and General and my father knew the Bible very well.

Bodrick shared he called my father "Holman," as several of the other friends called him William. Bodrick was in high school in the area and would visit my father and his friends at Claflin College on the weekends for a social charge. "It was a treasured time when I went to visit the group," he shared. Everyone in their group had an adopted name. The Orangeburg group was named the Lumumba Clan.

Gerald Mackie shared he and my father were friends for four years at Claflin, and a group of four of them, my father, King Fogle, General Thomas, and himself, were involved in activism together. He shared that my father always wore his trademark daishiki at Claflin. He recalled they served on a committee to "Save the Black College" and went to meetings together at a time when the federal government was considering reductions in funding to Black colleges.

"We were thick as thieves," shared King. The four of them were very close friends and shared unique experiences in college and were able to travel to different states and attend several conferences with the support of the college president and school's station wagon. They were able to learn more about the world and activism during their travels. They attended the African Liberation conferences in 1972 and 1973, and conferences in Little Rock, AR, and Shaw University, to name a few. I saw an archive from 1971 where my father and King attended a Student National Education Association with others from Claflin.

The four of them stayed in touch after graduation, and my father and King applied to graduate school at Atlanta University, where both were accepted into the Political Science department. King shared with me their story of how when they arrived at Atlanta University there was not a financial aid packet for them or housing. They thought their finances would have been handled similarly to how it was at Claflin and they would only need a small amount of money to attend, but that was not the case. When attending Claflin, they both received scholarships and Pell Grants and were involved in Upward Bound, where most of their college expenses were paid for except a few hundred dollars. At Atlanta University, they did not have an Upward Bound administrator to provide their financial package or scholarships to support their college expenses.

They had to make the tough decision to return home to Holly Hill, SC, and Orangeburg, SC where King was from. They only had $700 between the two of them when they arrived at Atlanta University, and that was only enough for one of them to attend a semester, and then they could apply for financial aid the next semester. They decided not to split, but to return home and return to the school after they had the funds to pay for it. They considered finding jobs in Atlanta to make money for school but didn't have a place to stay. They found jobs back home and stayed in touch with each other.

My father married my mom in 1974, and I was born in August 1975. King returned to Atlanta University in August 1975, and my parents remained in Holly Hill where my father worked and studied for the LSAT, the law school admissions exam. Mom started her first teaching job at a local school shortly after I was born. It was sad that my father would never return to Atlanta University or take his LSAT.

## Adult Years

He was described as an awesome friend by Rev.Jerome Clark and kind of protective. Jerome Clark shared that he admired him in some ways and would talk with him and that my father always had a good answer for him.

Rev. Clark helped my father with farming and was in a group that he took to Lake City, SC to help my mom's father with tobacco. My grandfather on my mom's side, Eugene Fleming Sr, was a sharecropper and also did seasonal work like construction. He would have people come to help in his fields during the year.

## Community Involvement

*"He was one of those persons who wanted to do better, make the world a better place." Aunt Missy*

Uncle Earnest described my father as "an analytical and brainy person, humanitarian, civic, and community involvement along with his other Claflin friends– King, Clarence, and your mom." He shared that my father enjoyed getting the younger ones involved in the community.

## His hobbies or Interests

It was great to hear about my father's interests and hobbies. He enjoyed playing games, and cards. My father and mother would play cards with Aunt

Olivia and Uncle Lymus. I learned about his love for books and Black History. He enjoyed talking about subjects and sharing opinions about several things. I recall a picture in our family album that shows my father leaning forward talking with family. I could see my Aunts and Uncle Earnest in the picture. He is talking and smiling. I can imagine several similar scenes like this of him engaging in conversations with family and friends on various topics.

*My father and Uncle Earnest enjoying a game of Scramble with my Aunt Mary Lee ( now deceased) looking on in the background.*

I learned he liked BBQ and nuts. Some of Granddaddy's sisters had pecan trees, and Cousin Adam shared they would eat nuts a lot from them. He loved basketball and baseball. I had no idea he played or enjoyed sports. His friend King Fogle shared, they were both big sports fans and played on the softball team at college. He shared my father was a Willie Mayes fan. Uncle Harold also shared that my father liked baseball. It was fascinating to learn all these new facts about my father and his interests.

Aunt Lula shared that Langston Hughes was his favorite poet.

I learned he enjoyed playing marbles and reading the Bible, according to Aunt Lula and Uncle Harold shared he liked to teach Sunday School to the Young Adults.

Uncle Odell shared that he enjoyed fishing a few times and recalled fishing with him. Uncle Odell also shared that my father loved Snickers candy bars. Understanding my father's interests continued to help connect the dots for me of the person he was, and it was all so valuable for me to learn. I loved Snicker bars too! It was wonderful to have more spaces filled with more knowledge and understanding of my father.

Aunt Missy shared that he liked to read and worked to improve his vocabulary and use of words, talked about business with his friends, and discussed ways to build a better community.

Cousin Vernon shared that my father liked reading, playing "country" baseball, knew a lot of football statistics, and had several discussions with their cousin Richard Sweatman on football. Cousin Vernon described their conversations as similar to commentators, reminding him of ESPN commentator Stephen A. Smith.

**Marriage**

*" The short time was good," my Mom shared.*

*My parent's wedding picture in 1974.*

I could hear through the stories and interviews the love my parents shared and the love my father had for my mother and me. It was beautiful to hear and see the love they shared.

Mom told me my father was tall, dark, and had white teeth. Most of his library, according to my mom, was Black authors and the Bible. He loved to study and read to me before I was born.

My parents met at Claflin College, now Claflin University, during their sophomore year in 1972. He was a Social Studies major, and she was an Education major. They dated for 2 ½ years before getting married in 1974. My father proposed to her in college.

They liked to go to the park and my mother shared he spent a lot of time with me and his father and family. He was smart in many areas. According to mom, he was very knowledgeable and knew the Bible from front to back. They had a wonderful marriage and relationship. I heard this in the interviews. The love they had for each other, the love my father had for me, and the time he took with me really speak to my father's character.

*My parents enjoying time together.*

"He had a great relationship with your Mom and was a good son and great person." Aunt Olivia Holman

Uncle Harold said that my father, "Loved his baby girl and his baby girl Mama," and that "Dorothy (my mom) loved him too."

Jerome Clark shared he enjoyed my parent's relationship and that my father was an awesome husband.

Aunt Missy shared that my father was a very caring, loving, and protective husband. She shared he was very helpful with household responsibilities and it was a joint effort to take care of things together with my mom.

*My mom and father during college.*

### Fatherhood – His Love for Me

*"Your Dad really loved you. He was very proud of you when you were born. He was a great father." Aunt Olivia*

*A picture of me as a baby.*

I heard this similar theme from all the family and friends I spoke to of the great love he had for me and my mom and his family. It warmed my heart so much to see and hear about the amount of great love he had for me and the time he took with me during the short time we had together. Hearing those words and knowing the great amount of love he shared with me brings me great joy.

"Couldn't find a better one. He was always doing something for his baby girl." Aunt Lula

Aunt Lula and Uncle Harold shared how much he loved his baby girl and that I was his "heartbeat." They shared he was doting on me when my mom was pregnant with me and that he was a very good father and very protective of his family. Aunt Lula shared, "He provided well for his family."

Jerome Clark shared that my father was a great father to me. It was great to hear how much my father loved me and the time he spent with me.

Aunt Missy shared my father was "crazy about his little baby."

## Music

I really wanted to understand if he had a love of music and who his favorite artists were. I remember seeing a quote as a child that said, *"Music is the universal language"*.

Mom told me that my father listened to all types of music, which included gospel, the early 70s, some country, and just "good music". My uncles shared he enjoyed R&B music, and Uncle Harold shared that Otis Redding was one of his favorite singers. Cousin Adam Brown shared that my father and my Uncle Harold introduced him to rock music and to Jimi Hendrix.

Aunt Lula shared that my father could sing and also liked gospel music and the old hymns. She shared that his favorite hymn he would sing was "Are you Able, said the Master".

A fond memory Cousin Vernon shared was one day riding with my father and their cousin Richard Sweatman. There was a song on the radio that he recalled they played that he never heard before. I googled the only phrase he could recall during our interview, which was "Been a long time." I played the song that came up from Google, and this was a song by the group New Birth from 1972, and Cousin Vernon shared that was, in fact, the song. They gave him a Colt 45 for the first time. He shared that this beer took a toll on his stomach. He recalled that story recently when talking with someone and shared that was one of his fondest memories with my father. We laughed when he shared this story.

It was great to see how much my father enjoyed music and different types of music. This was another connection point for me to learn more about him. It was fascinating to hear these stories.

## Challenges

*"He weathered the storm through all that and kept his dignity."* Uncle Harold

Like all of us, my father faced challenges in his life. Three of the key challenges he faced were living in the South, living in Holly Hill, and the limitations placed on Black people at that time. He had a difficult time finding a job in his field of study after graduating from college. I heard in a few interviews that he experienced some challenges directed towards him by some for being so intelligent. Like each of us, he had to navigate the challenges that life may send our way.

He was born in 1950 in rural South Carolina. The world and state were different then. Racial segregation was present, and times were tough for Black Americans and even more challenging in the South. My grandfather managed farm workers, and my father, uncle, and other family members helped him manage and run his business. Cousin Adam shared they sold watermelon, wood, and vegetables. These are some of the challenges shared by family:

· Being poor at that time. "We always had food, vegetables, and fruit," Peter Holman

· "He couldn't get a job in his field when he graduated from college." Aunt Sue

She also shared likely finances while in college were challenging for him.

· "Living in the South at that time." Aunt Olivia

· "Trying to make it and move forward after graduation in Holly Hill." Rodney Holman

"William had a strong personality, so I couldn't tell if there were other challenges." Adam Brown

"He wanted to get out (of Holly Hill) and do more. He wanted to get out and help Granddaddy at the same time." Cousin Vernon

My father was employed as a dispatcher at the local police department in Holly Hill after college. He would continue to help his father with his farming business during this time also.

I can not fully imagine the impact and strain these challenges had on my father during his life. I was glad to learn, as Uncle Harold mentioned, that he maintained his dignity through it all. My mom shared he desired to obtain his PhD.

**Fondest Memories and "What you remember most about him":**

*"His beautiful white teeth and his big smile." Aunt Lula*

He and cousin Maisy's son drove her and Uncle Lymus back to South Carolina from Fort Benning in Georgia shared Aunt Olivia.

"When we would come to visit, he was happy to see us." Peter Holman

Swimming in the pond behind Aunt Margaret Williams' house was the fondest memory shared by Cousin Adam Brown. This experience was a unique one and brought both of us to laughter. Adam shared it was him, my father and the five Williams boys that decided to go swimming one day. They took off their clothes and swam in the pond without any bathing suits, played games, and laughed. That was a very "carefree time" for them, shared Cousin Adam, and the "world was their oyster." Cousin Adam and I laughed at this story so hard.

Uncle Harold said there was "the quiet air about his face." He also said his son Haileab has the same type of quietness to his face and reminds him of my father.

Aunt Lula recalled a time when a fly landed in my father's cup of coffee, and instead of pouring out the coffee, my father threw the fly out and continued to drink his coffee. "He was different," she shared and we all laughed at this memory.

Uncle Harold's fondest memory was during a trip to Jackson, Mississippi with my father and Aunt Sue. My father asked if they wanted to buy any dry fruit at the beginning of the trip, and they said no, but as the trip went along, they started getting hungry and ran out of food. That's when my father turned around and looked at them and started eating his dry fruit. We all had to laugh at this because he offered them at the beginning of the trip, and then when all their food was gone, it was too late, and he didn't share any of his dry fruit with them. That was hilarious. Aunt Lula, Uncle Harold, and I laughed at this story.

Aunt Minnie shared a memory of my father and Uncle Odell attending her brother's funeral in 1974 and giving a flower to the family. She remembered the thoughtfulness of them attending and recalled hearing when the card was read that it was from William Holman, classmate, and Odell Holman. She believed that my father purchased the flower and felt it was thoughtful of them to attend the funeral.

Aunt Missy shared it was when they would compete and challenge each other with the use of words and vocabulary. She also shared a fond memory of when my father worked as hard as everyone else in the Fleming family, ( my mom's siblings), at clearing "new ground" for their family plot of land for building a house on. "He worked with us like he had vested interest. There was never a time he stood off like a stranger and always helped and worked like everyone else," she shared.

Uncle Earnest: "His affectionate smile, very playful, makes you smile. Brighten up your day and was a happy-go-lucky person." He shared you couldn't sit around him and not smile.

Bodrick shared it was, sitting around the dorm room at Claflin College and talking with my father and friends. "Holman was one of those people. His presentation was captivating." He recalled how my father could develop a full argument and make it very understandable and shared in a positive way an analysis of their situation. The conversations he shared went beyond Orangeburg and the college campus. He shared they were "all brothers in the movement." He described my father as having a "depth of understanding, a true political scientist, and his personal focus was captivating and spoke in a conversational and relaxed tone."

# Chapter 9- The Power of Love and His Goals and Dreams

**Love Never Dies**

*"William Lee being William Lee. He could sense a lot and didn't favor folks and treat all the same," said Cousin Vernon.*

There is an undeniable truth that the love we share for our loved ones who die never goes away. I could see and hear the love my father's friends and family had for him when I talked with each of them. I could still see the pain they experienced by his sudden death at 26 ½ years old. They expressed that he left a void in their lives that never went away.

One of my most touching interviews was with my Uncle Odell. This interview was particularly touching to me as I could see and hear that there was a lot of grief and pain still present for my uncle. I am thankful that he took the time with Aunt Minnie to share his memories of my father with me.

Tears were shed during some of the interviews I made. We also enjoyed moments of laughter and joy during our interviews. It was a process that allowed me to learn so much about my father and my family. I am thankful for the opportunity to capture and share the memories and love so many people had for my father. Typically, I would space the interviews out a few days or schedule one a week, but on a couple of occasions, I had two interviews on two consecutive days. One of these occasions was when I interviewed Aunt Lula and Uncle Odell on back-to-back days.

As I approached these final two interviews with two of my father's youngest siblings, I could not have imagined the joy and emotional impact these final interviews would have on me. It was indeed one of the most touching interviews I had, and necessary to share the great memories my uncle and aunt shared. I learned more about my father's childhood, teenage years, and early adult years. I learned about his hobbies more, and even his nickname and nicknames he gave my Uncle Odell and so many more pieces of his personality and life. I am thankful to conclude this portion of the interviews with my father's siblings. My aunts and uncles, cousins, close friends, and my mom helped me gain such a great understanding and picture of my father, from his personality and spirit to his hopes and dreams. It was such an amazing experience.

I was amazed, too, when I asked everyone I spoke to outside of my immediate family when they first met my father, and they all quickly shared the year or time in school when they first met him.

**My Father's Goals and Dreams**

*"He wanted to get his Ph.D., and we wanted to move to Orangeburg. He wanted a lot for his parents and a better life."* Mom

It was important to me to understand my father's goals and dreams as a way to further understand him and the future he hoped his life to become. I wanted to understand what he was working towards for his life. I asked family and friends about his goals and dreams, and this is what I learned from our discussions.

Mom shared they had already picked out the general location for where they wanted to move to and had enough money for the down payment. She still recalls the area they were planning to live in. This was so surprising to me to hear and so sad at the same time, that he didn't live long enough for them to move there.

Some interviewed shared he would have likely been a lawyer, political scientist, or college professor. I enjoyed hearing what they shared about his dreams, goals or hopes.

"I think he would have gone far. He was beyond South Carolina at that time." Aunt Olivia Holman

"A scholar. He wanted to do better, do better for his family." Rodney Holman

Cousin Rodney didn't think my father really wanted to be in Holly Hill, but his life ended before he was able to move from the area.

King shared my father would have been a political scientist and that he was interested in law.

Aunt Lula, Aunt Minnie and Uncle Odell shared he wanted to be a lawyer. Uncle Harold shared he was "always defending things."

"He would love to see you have your own business and make a positive difference for others. That was his dream to make a positive difference." Aunt Missy

She also shared that my father and his group of friends all dreamed of making positive changes where they lived; they wanted to change hearts, change mindsets and make a difference.

Cousin Vernon shared my father was the only child out of his family to go to college. "Going to college was his dream," Cousin Vernon said. He shared that my father had a lot of knowledge.

Uncle Earnest shared that my parents and their close friends ( King Fogle and Clarence Burke) were working on a project, endowment, or scholarship. Another goal he shared was to be a role model for the younger generation and be involved in civic duties. "He wanted to contribute to society," Uncle Earnest shared.

Bodrick: "I think he would be a college professor, analyst, or writer." He shared my father was not shy and would have been a voice if he was still here. "He would be well-rounded, having that level of influence and exposure to people for what he had to offer."

"Liberation of Black people across the nation; justice and equality for people across the nation," shared Gerald Mackie.

These were awesome goals my father had. He desired to make a difference in the world and help the next generation through Black liberation, becoming a lawyer and obtaining his PhD. This gives me another view of where he desired to go next in his life before his untimely death. This helps share the impact and influence he desired to have in the world.

**The Power of Memories**

*"Being a person with a vision, he could get things done and trying to bring others along. He tried to help everyone ( church, family, community)." my Mom*

Memories are powerful. Growing up, I was always told my father died when I was around 2 or 2 1/2 years old. After looking again at my father's obituary, I noticed he died in January 1977. My birthday is in August, so my father died before I was two years old and closer to when I was a year and a half old. This was significant and surprising that I only spent one birthday with my father. I am thankful we have pictures together during my first one and a half years of life. I am thankful to have pictures of my first birthday, for every picture we took together, and every memory and moment shared during this short time. I am thankful to hear about the love he shared with me and my mom during the time he was with us. I am thankful to have experienced my father's love and heard how proud he was of me.

*My first birthday picture with my parents.*

As I write this section for the book, tears of joy flow down my face. There is such power in understanding the power of love, and our memories help us to fully understand how much we mean to others and how much they love us. We have a wonderful opportunity in our lives to share memories of our loved ones with each other to help us know more about those we have loved and lost, to help heal wounds of loss and sadness, and to provide insights into our family's joys, and pains.

This journey to learn more about my father has helped me learn more about myself, too. This journey has helped me grow stronger emotionally and fully understand the love he shared with me and the bond we shared during the time he lived. The bond we shared continued as I grew up. I was very protective of keeping his memory alive and never once thought about calling my stepfather "Dad", out of respect for my father, after my mom re-married. I even considered keeping my maiden name after I married my husband to continue with my father's legacy but decided to take on my husband's last name.

This process has brought me closer to my father and allowed me to learn more about who he was as a person, father, husband, friend, son, and sibling. It has been one of the best gifts I could give him and myself to further capture and share his legacy and love with others, particularly our family.

# Chapter 10 - My Father's Death

**Duality of Life and Death, Grief and Joy**

*"When he died, it hurt me to my heart. It was very difficult." Adam Brown*

Cousin Adam's words capture how many felt and the essence felt by friends and family. I decided not to ask anyone who was interviewed about my father's death and would only capture what they shared with me. I knew how difficult it was for them to share memories of him with me , as was evident by the tears shared at times, and I could notice some still experienced grief of his sudden passing. In several interviews, my father's death was mentioned by the person I was interviewing.

Some of the memories of his death included where they were when they heard the news. Some shared they arrived at the scene of the accident and what they observed or the impact of what they saw. I realized that trauma and pain from over forty years were still present.

Mom suppressed a lot of her pain and had to raise me as a single mother until she remarried when I was 10. I am not sure how other family members managed their grief, but I could see through the time I spent with each person I interviewed that there were remnants of grief and pain still present. There was joy present with each person also. Each person had great memories to share with me, and my father left such a lasting mark on each of their lives. They each shared loving stories with me about the person he was and how he was easy to get along with, very protective of his family, and well-mannered to his parents. Everyone shared such a loving family and friend relationship with my father. I am honored to carry on my father's legacy and share his life, accomplishments, love, and the impact he made on family, friends and the community.

**Death**

*"You had a phenomenal Dad," shared his friend Gerald Mackie.*

Several of the family and friends shared different memories of his death and how it impacted them. I didn't even ask any follow-up questions when they spoke about my father's death; I just listened to everything they shared. There was still some shock and confusion shared by some when recalling their memories of that day in January 1977 in Eutawville, SC, when my father died in a car accident. Some family members went to the scene of my father's accident. Some people that I spoke to remembered and shared where they were when they heard the message of his death. Some I interviewed spoke with my father on his final day on earth before his accident. One person had a vision of his death and funeral church seating before it occurred.

Aunt Sue recalls talking with my father that morning when she called my grandmother's house, and my father answered the phone. She still recalls their final conversation to this day. She shared he would often return their car with little gas. Their conversation sounded like, "This is You," she said, and he said, "Yeah, next time I borrow y'all car I'll make sure I have some gas in it." They continued to talk a bit further and Aunt Sue shared she would tease him about how he always would bring the car back empty. This was such a distinct moment when I spoke with Aunt Sue, and her ability to recall their last conversation blew me away, and it was touching.

***When they learned he was in a car accident or had died:***

*"When it happened, it took a piece out of my life." Uncle Harold*

Mom was at work at the local St. James elementary school in Eutawville, and someone came to her classroom door to let her know about the accident. She shared that she couldn't believe something else could happen after losing several other close family members the year before, one of these close family members was her mother. My mom went to the scene of the accident.

King Fogle shared he was on his college campus on a cold day, and a friend James Carew told him about the accident.

Uncle Harold told me he had returned from work, and someone shared the news with him that his brother-in-law had died in an accident and offered to give him a ride home.

Uncle Harold said he didn't realize how close he and my father were or how much time they spent around each other until this happened.

Aunt Lula shared she had returned from work and shared the name of the place where she worked and had gone to the grocery store. She was told the news and left the grocery store. She shared with me that my father had been working that day hauling wood and had visited my mom at the school that day.

Aunt Olivia shared she and Uncle Lymus were in Germany when they received the news and had to return home to the states.

Cousin Rodney was about 14 or 15 when my father died. He arrived at the scene of the accident and recalled what he saw that day.

Uncle Odell shared he went to the spot where my father was killed. "It hurt me so much because he was my older brother." Uncle Odell shared the bond they had and how he would follow my father around growing up. Uncle Odell shared that talking about him for this book "opened up a lot of raw wounds."

This statement was so true, and I could feel it in our discussions and other discussions with family members. There were still wounds of my father's loss that they were dealing with. As Uncle Odell shared, Aunt Minnie and I agreed with, "Grieving never goes away."

I can't imagine arriving at the scene to see your loved one injured and then declared dead. That memory alone would be so much and too much to process and begin to heal from.

Aunt Sue, Uncle Joe, and my Mom all arrived at the scene of the accident. There likely were several other family members present also but these few I am mentioning by name. Aunt Sue shared she saw my father. "He was sitting up behind the wheel, but he was gone."

Uncle Joe shared that the tree my father's truck struck remained along Highway 104 until recently. It has since been cut down.

"It was so much pain. It was so much. So painful," Mom shared.

She blocked several memories from her mind to be able to cope and manage life after my father's death. She shared that people didn't go to grief counseling in the 1970s like they do now. I observe now that she tried to suppress her grief and move forward the best way she could.

"It was just a time because it was sudden," said Aunt Sue. "We had a good relationship."

"Time was just too short," one of my Uncles shared during our interview.

There was a combination of expressions that the time with my father was too short across some of the interviews, and also, there was an awareness and acceptance that God's timing is not our timing and that God has a perfect plan for each of us. Two of my aunts shared so beautifully that my father's legacy lives on through me and my sons and is shared by others, which is so true!! It's a beautiful thing to know that our loved ones can have a legacy that lives beyond their time here on earth.

Cousin Peter shared he never understood that accident and that it bothered him a lot.

"Gone too soon," shared Aunt Missy, and she said, "Our ways are not God's ways and that God makes no mistakes."

Cousin Vernon shared my father was close to his father, Uncle Sing, and recalled he was upset about my father's death. Cousin Vernon is six years younger than my father.

Bodrick shared he was in Pittsburgh, Pennsylvania, in his first year of college when my father died and didn't know about his funeral. "I regret I was not there," he shared.

Gerald Mackie shared that my mother shared with him about my father's death and recalled I was about two years old.

*My father's picture from his obituary. It has been kept in a photo album folded all these years.*

# Chapter 11- A Void in the Family and Filling the Gap

**God Makes no Mistakes**

*"Grieving never goes away." Uncle Odell*

God makes no mistakes is something my Grandma Eva shared with me one day when we talked about my father when I was younger. I can't remember my age when we had that particular conversation, but I remember the end of one of her sentences saying that God doesn't make any mistakes when we were talking about my father. I could imagine this statement brought peace to my Grandmother as she was still processing the loss of her son. This statement would provide peace to me at different times in my life when grief, sadness, or longing to understand why things turned out the way they did with my father passing at such a young age and me not having the opportunity to really know him further or remember him. I had to remember him by pictures, some facts and comments shared by my family, and over time, different items he owned that my mom shared with me after I was an adult. I have some of his writings, his class ring, and his police badge, so my goal is to help fill in the missing pieces of the memory and life of my father with this book. I will continue this journey to learn more about my father and share his life with others and the world.

*My grandma( Eva Holman) during a visit to Nebraska to visit Uncle Lymus.*

In the 70's and 80's, there was not much talk within my family of loved ones that passed. So, the void I felt was never really filled with understanding or learning more about my father during that time. There was no grief counselor back then that I visited to process my feelings of loss and being different as a child who lost their parent. It was such a different time. I adjusted the best ways I knew and managed the best way I knew and the best way I knew to navigate this most unusual situation I found myself in. Some people in my circles growing up knew my father was deceased. Most people likely didn't know because I am a private type of person with family relationships and, in particular, regarding loss.

I remember one of my friends in high school asking another one of my friends– if they didn't know that my father was deceased. I remember being asked by my hairstylist, Val, in Delaware once very gracefully what about my father since I talked a lot about my mother, and I then shared, "My father is deceased and died when I was very young, about two years old." It was a side of my story that was very sad and painful to share. So much that I didn't share it with people outside of family unless I knew them well, and, of course, if they asked me about it. I was in a group I had not volunteered for and had no control or choice in the outcome but had to learn how to accept the hand I was dealt and continue to move forward.

### Filling in the Gap

*"My sister needed me, and I went." Uncle Levern Fleming ( Uncle Bubba)*

I was reminded when interviewing Uncle Levern Fleming (Uncle Bubba) of the key role he played following my father's death when he stayed with my mom and me until she was able to move back home. My mom was a school teacher at the time of my father's death and had to finish her school term. Uncle Bubba started filling in the gap during that time for us. I remember Mom sharing that he stayed with us until we moved back to Lake City but talking with my uncle helped make this time period clearer to me. He left his home, and his girlfriend at the time and went to Holly Hill to live with us before we moved. He shared with me that he cooked, cleaned, and took care of me during that time. To further put it into perspective, he shared that I "just started walking good" when he moved in with us. These additional details my uncle shared about this period of time with me were precious and provided a unique perspective and showed the immediate ways he helped fill the gap for my mom and me following my father's death.

My mom later shared with me while I was writing this book during one of our several discussions, that she drove to Eutawville after we moved back to Lake City for a few months to complete her teaching contract to finish the school year. It was shocking to learn that she drove over an hour each way 5 days/week for a few months while grieving and raising me to complete her teaching contract for that school year. I saw my mom's strength in such a different way. I can't even imagine what it took for her to do this and how important it really was for others to help fill in the gap for us during this time and while I was growing up.

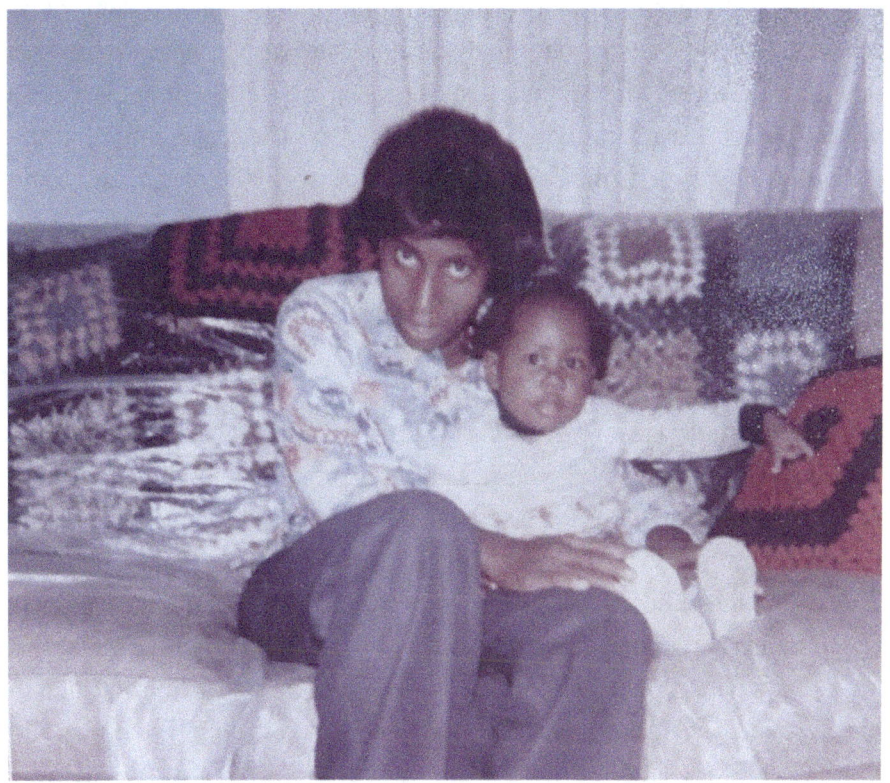

*Me and Mom enjoying time together.*

As long as I can remember, I stayed connected with my father's side of the family – the Holmans mainly because my mom made sure that I spent time visiting my family when I was growing up at least four times during the year. We lived about 1.5 hours away. As a child of the '70s and '80s, this felt a long way away. There were less ways available to stay in touch back then from this distance, compared to the many different ways available through technology today, but we were able to do that. This was before the time of the Internet or Facetime, so seeing each other in person or calling on the phone was how we best connected with family that was not in the same area or around the corner from us. I would stay with my grandparents and be able to visit my aunts, uncles, and cousins and attend church with my grandparents and visit my extended family during these times, meeting distant cousins, some older (Cousin Maisy who always had candy to share and was so sweet) to younger cousins. There were a lot of cousins and family to meet. I would say everyone pretty much knew my grandparents, Adam (Mix) and Eva Holman, in the Holly Hill, SC area that I met, as they were very active in their local church and community.

I am thankful to my family on the Holman side for always taking time with me when I visited during the years. Even though I didn't grow up every day with my family on the Holman side, I always felt connected to my cousins, aunts and uncles, and grandparents. Aunt Lula said she was thankful my mom allowed me to stay close to them. I didn't realize any parents would not have kept their children close to both sides of their families after their spouse died. I always thought that it would be expected to keep me in connection with my family as family is so important on my mother's side of the family too.

When I think of how my family on both the Fleming, my mom's side, and the Holman side supported me during my childhood, I am eternally grateful. My father's parents and Mom's Dad (Granddaddy) were so loving and kind to me. My aunts and uncles stayed involved in my life from both my father's and mother's sides. They were invested in my education and how I was doing. I remember graduating from high school, and my aunts and uncles from the Holman side came to graduation to join us. I always felt supported and that is due to all my family who helped fill the gap for me when I was growing up without a father. My family from both of my parent's sides attended my wedding, baby showers, and my children's birthday parties and have stayed connected in my life.

I had good father figures who tried to fill in for me during life as a child growing up and as an adult. I am thankful for my grandfathers, uncles, stepfather (Walter), and friends of the family. I remember going to ask my Uncle Abraham ( Fleming) whether or not to pursue a Co-Op in college. He advised me to stay in school and work after graduating college. I valued his guidance, listened to him, and chose not to take the Co-Op opportunity and continue in school. My stepfather's brother, Johnny, helped me learn how to drive a car. I reminded him recently that I still remembered this.

I was able to spend time and visit my uncles' families and be taken places with them or ask them questions and learn nuggets of wisdom. My aunts were fantastic and played a critical role as I grew up. I remember visiting Aunt Missy and having sleepovers at her house with my cousins. I always had cousins around growing up (some were my mother's age) and some younger closer to my age and younger. I have always experienced a loving family from grandparents, aunts, uncles, cousins, and more! This ability for family to help close the gap was critical to me growing up and though my father was no longer there, they made sure that I had what I needed and enjoyed the comforts of family.

*A picture with me, my Granddaddy ( Eugene Fleming, Sr. -my Mom's father) and cousin Joanne in Lake City SC.*

I remember only one time when I visited my grandparents on my father's side (Adam "Mix" and Eva) that I asked to go back home. I was a little girl, maybe around five years old. I told Grandma I wanted to go home and being the wonderful and loving grandma she was, she called my mom, let me talk to her, told my mom that I wanted to go home, and Mom came to get me. I can't remember, but my Uncle Bubba may have traveled with my mom to get me.

I lived about an hour and a half away from my grandparents, and I don't know why I wanted to go home, but I just did. I went back home, and no one fussed at me, and I didn't get in trouble. The family was understanding and kind that way. After some months, I returned to my grandparents' house and stayed the whole trip. I don't remember asking to return home early again. I always loved visiting my grandparents and visiting and playing with my cousins and seeing my aunts, uncles, and extended family. My grandfather would drive so slowly, but family and church were the center of their lives. They took me everywhere with them when I visited; sometimes I would visit my aunts and spend the day and overnight. They did a great job taking me to church, showing me their Christian faith, and sharing it with me in words and actions. They loved me completely like they did all their grandchildren. They made me feel at home every time I visited, and I would meet different family members. So though I lived an hour and a half away, I always stayed close to my father's family and could still grow up knowing them (immediate and some extended family). I learned later in life that this type of dynamic of staying in touch and close after the death of a parent or spouse is not as common as I thought it would be.

My life would not be complete without my cousins and family on the Holman side. I treasure my father's side of the family as much as my mother's side, and I am thankful to my mom and my father's family for keeping me close to them and allowing me the opportunity to know them as I grew up and spend precious time with my grandparents that hold a very special place in my heart and whose picture I have on my wall today in my living room. My grandma kept me in the loop on family matters and updates, so I was kept informed of family happenings though I lived away from the rest of the Holmans. As I got older, my grandma would call me, as well as my other first cousins, about every two weeks, at least once a month, until her health got worse. I am thankful for the role everyone played in keeping this family connection and bond for me. I have continued these connections with my children, bringing them to family reunions and visits on the Holman side to ensure they know and meet their great-aunts, uncles, and cousins in the Holman family.

*Uncle Bubba was one of the many family members that filled in the gap for me and my Mom.*

# Chapter 12- His Legacy Lives On

**My Father's Legacy**

*"His legacy lives on." Aunt Lula*

When I think of legacy, I think of what remains or continues after we are no longer here. The remaining impact we make or have on others as well. The difference our lives have made for others, our community, or the world. I asked family and friends what my father was best known for, and they shared many things with me. Some of the key areas I heard several times connected to his drive and goals, love and kindness, knowledge, and fight for social justice and equality.

**His drive and goals:**

*"He tried to be successful." Peter Holman*

Cousin Vernon shared my father was "always striving to do better." He shared he would question you to do better and "make you feel better as a person." He added my father was appreciative and would reach out to help others. He shared he was honest, good, and tried to do right.

**His love and kindness:**

*"His kindness and love for people, he liked people and prided himself on getting along with others." Adam Brown*

Aunt Missy: "He was a stand-up guy. A very caring person, who wanted the best for his family, he wanted to better himself." She shared that his legacy lives on, and others can see that he did something positive with his life so they can do the same.

## His knowledge

*"Very knowledgeable of Black History and tired to educate others and get people involved."* Gerald Mackie

Jerome Clark: "He was a thinker, his intelligence and philosopher."

"You made a significant impact . He would be so, so proud of his grandsons. They are hard workers," shared Aunt Missy.

## His fight for Social Justice and Equality

*"He was for equal justice, regardless of your skin color."* Cousin Vernon

"He was real," said Cousin Vernon. He shared that my father would have been proud of how I grew up and who I have become.

"He wanted the best for his fellow persons, especially you." Uncle Earnest. My uncle also shared my father would want me to continue to build and add on whatever he started in his life.

Bodrick: "He was quite a gentleman." He shared that what was unique to him about my father was that "he could use his voice, knew how to captivate when explaining and sharing knowledge, as he talked and communicated. He was demonstrative."

Uncle Joe shared that my father "tried his best to get me to be the Superintendent of the Sunday School." He refused at first, but following my father's death, he became the Superintendent of the Sunday School at Galilee Christian Church in Holly Hill, SC.

After my father's passing, his college friends General Thomas, Clarence Burke, and King Fogel decided to meet annually. King said they started these meetings in 1979 and continued for several years. I remembered attending these when I was growing up, too, so everyone could stay connected and see each other and their families. They all continued to contribute to the liberation of black people in their own ways and included others they met in college to extend this circle of friends.

## I asked the family members I interviewed if anyone reminded them of my father in the family.

*"He lived a very quality life. He got a lot of things done while he was here. He*

*would want for all of us to add on and move these forward," Uncle Earnest shared.*

Some shared names of the people that reminded them of my father and what main traits or characteristics they shared with my father.

"Lymus reminded me of William Lee, and they reminded me of each other and also Granddaddy," shared Cousin Vernon. He also shared that the actor Louis Gossett Jr. reminds him of my father a lot in little ways, of how he talks, his height, how he carries himself, and his laugh. He mentioned a particular movie, "An Officer and Gentleman," from the 1980s, where he saw some similarities. I remember this movie and will have to watch it again to observe some of the similarities Cousin Vernon mentioned. I can recall Louis Gossett Jr. being tall, and dark, and playing dignified roles in movies.

At least three or four family members told me that my cousin Haileab Samuel reminds them of my father in his appearance, personality, thought patterns, and level of thinking. Aunt Minnie told me that Haileab's smile, even tone and speech, reminds her of how my father spoke.

Cousin Vernon also shared that my cousin Haileab reminds him of my father. He shared that Haileab talks like my father, and has similar mannerisms, voice, and identical smile. He told Haileab that he reminds him a lot of William Lee. He shared that both of them, when they talk to you, "make you feel like you are important."

My youngest son Nathan reminds my Uncle Odell and Aunt Minnie of my father. When I shared a picture of me and Nathan with a few family and friends I interviewed over the phone, they agreed that he looks like his grandfather. Aunt Olivia shared that I reminded her of him because of our common traits – being kind, loyal, extremely intelligent, and down to earth with everyone.

Aunt Lula shared I have my father's spirit and internal qualities. Uncle Harold shared I have his mannerisms and intellect.

I still recall Uncle Lymus sharing when I was a teenager, when I visited him and his family in Nebraska along with many of the Holmans, that I had "quiet confidence" like my father.

Cousin Peter shared that the two of them had similarities. They both were policemen. My father was a dispatcher, and Peter was a policeman in Summerville, SC, the first Black policeman who worked for the town of

Summerville. They both worked for change and civil rights in different ways. Peter shared he was quiet when he was younger before going to Vietnam. He shared he was also studious like my father.

Cousin Adam Brown shared that Uncle Lymus Holman (now deceased) reminded him of my father, and my father reminded him of Uncle Lymus. Uncle Lymus was one of my father's older brothers and six years older . "They were cut out of the same cloth and got along so well. William knew what Lymus was thinking." shared Cousin Adam Brown.

*My grandparents ( Adam and Eva Holman).*

Cousin Adam also told me that my father was similar to Granddad (Adam Holman) with his hard work and ability to hustle, motivate others, and make money. He felt he had a similar ability to Grandma (Eva Holman) when communicating. He could " share what needed to be said in his way," whether positive or negative updates.

Rodney Holman: "No one compares to William Lee and your mother for me. To this day, I still miss him dearly."

**Some additional similarities my father and I share**

*"He wanted to contribute to society," Uncle Earnest shared of my father.*

As I talked with family and friends about my father and looked at his old yearbooks from high school and college, I noticed many similarities. My father was a Social Studies major in college and President of his college Social Studies club, I saw newspaper archives from *The Times and Democrat* (Orangeburg, South Carolina) from 1971 and 1973. I also loved Social Studies and took a strong interest in Black History for as long as I can remember. I was active in the Corporate Black Employee network when I was in Corporate America and am now active with diversity, equity, and inclusion initiatives in my local Chamber of Commerce.

We both liked speaking and writing/journalism. My father was the editor of his high school yearbook, and I was the editor of my high school newsletter. I competed in oratorical contests in high school and speak today for different groups and as a part of my business. We both graduated cum laude from our colleges. We both really value family and can get along with pretty much anyone. We both enjoyed being a part of academic teams. I was on the Academic team in high school and one or two years in college. As I mentioned, my father was a member of the Independent Team that won the World Bowl several times in college. We both enjoyed this type of trivia and competition. We both love music and can sing. His legacy will continue to live on with me in ways I didn't know until writing this book. My children continue his legacy also today.

Near the end of writing this book, I saw newspaper archives of articles that mentioned my father in the *Times and Democrat* (Orangeburg, South Carolina) with the help of a wonderful person who works in the Carolina Room in the Florence, SC library. I asked the reference person for any documents related to my father in Orangeburg, SC, or Holly Hill, SC, from 1965 to 1977. The reference contact found about ten references to my father, under "William Lee Holman" or "William Holman" when she searched in Orangeburg, SC, or with Claflin College. I previously had one newspaper clipping from 1972 that highlighted my father and his friends who were a part of the Independent Team for the World Bowl.

I now have archives from 1971, during his time in college, until 1977 with his obituary. These pieces of history are invaluable and added another layer of legacy, love, and memories of my father! I saw images and updates that include his time as a member of the Claflin World Bowl Team, his activities as a part of the Social Studies Club at Claflin, a National Student meeting he attended along with his friend King Fogle in 1971, his honors at graduation (Cum Laude), the report of his death and his obituary printed in the newspaper.

I learned more details about his college experience and accomplishments. There were other documents that showed his introduction of a guest speaker and trips connected with the school. I learned some more details of his life and death on this day. I was very happy to learn these final details as I prepared to conclude this book. I realized at this point that I had gathered all the remaining details or articles I needed to move forward to finalize this dedication to my father's life, memory, and legacy. I was ready to work on completing the final sections of the book based on earlier interviews that I had completed. No additional research was needed as my father's life, love , and legacy have become clearer and more complete to me. I shared with my Mom and one of my friends the highlights of the articles I found and shared a few copies with my Mom that week for her keeping. I felt that I had completed the assignment to honor his life.

*Me and my father at home.*

# Chapter 13- Grief, Love and Lasting Memories

**It's Ok to Grieve**

*"People say you get over grief, but I never got over William,"* *shared Cousin* *Rodney.*

Cousin Rodney Holman's expression of his grief shares a similar feeling I heard when talking with friends and family. During the interviews I had with family and friends, I could see how some were still grieving the loss of my father and how challenging or sad sharing some memories was for some. I can see there was still grief present. Uncle Odell said he doesn't talk about my father because it hurts so bad.

When I talked with some, it took them some time during our discussion as they shared memories with me, and I gave them the space they needed to share what they could and desired to share with me.

Grief is mourning the loss of a loved one. Missing the time you lost with them and recalling the life and time spent together that have ended for now. Grief is a natural process necessary for us all to go through. In my family, I noticed that many family members still grieved the loss of my father, and I am aware that due to the drastic and sudden nature of his death, some may not have allowed themselves time to grieve. I have grieved his death my entire life. I can say that even with this amount of time, I had not fully grieved and had space to process the loss and void I experienced fully. I am thankful for this opportunity to complete the grieving process and continue to heal. My healing process may look different from someone else, and that's okay. My healing process is designed for me and will help make me whole again.

The little girl that went to the window every day for a long time now has a picture of her father more complete than ever before and a picture I can share with my children and hold dear in my heart forever. I now have happy memories to include in my memory bank along with the sad awareness of his sudden death and the years lost. I am happy to be able to learn more about who he was, how he lived, and the impact he made. I am honored to have met him at this time of my life and to see how and where he appears in my life. Today, I honor his life, love, and legacy with this book and provide an opportunity for others to share and speak about him in love and truth. He is greatly missed and his death shocked our family and his friends. I am grateful to have a father who loved me and loved his family and others. I am thankful to be able to grieve and rejoice simultaneously. I encourage others to be okay allowing themselves to grieve the loss of my father and other loved ones and to cherish the good times, love, memories shared, as they process the loss while honoring his memory and life.

*Little me in this picture.*

I am motivated to learn more about him and dedicate a lasting memory to his life and legacy. I am a part of his legacy and hope he would be proud of me today! For anyone who has not allowed yourself to grieve in the ways and waves you need, it's not too late to open your heart and allow yourself to grieve so you can heal and live a fuller life.

One of the final questions I asked during the interviews was how they thought my father would want to be remembered. It would be a great summary of my time talking with friends and family to hear how they thought my father would like to be remembered.

**Here is what I heard from our discussions, that he would want to be remembered as someone:**

Aunt Sue: "Person always fighting for justice, that the right thing would be done and people would be treated fairly. Good husband and father. "

King Fogle: "A person who had dreams, had vision, go to the extreme for others - changes for all, especially Black people. Somebody who loved his people and was prepared to do anything to liberate them. Total liberation of Black people here and around the world. Always looking for ways we could be totally free. One with an undying love for Black people. Dedicate his life to improving the life of our people."

Aunt Olivia: "Good, decent, kind, intelligent person that didn't look down on others. He stood for the little man."

Aunt Lula: "Humble vessel that God used. Intelligent, noticed by the Spirit to do what he can."

Aunt Lula also shared that "he was spiritual, knew what he knew and was confident."

Uncle Harold: "William Lee, Mix Holman's son, designated for the political side and church."

Uncle Odell: "Very kind and caring person and loved everybody; wasn't hard to get along with. Treated others like he would treat his family. He had a loving spirit."

Earline McClary: "Person who worked hard, wanted to see change in the world, he really wanted to see change in the world." Aunt Earline shared that my father and his friends felt they could change the world and were committed to making a positive difference.

Vernon Williams: "As a good friend, father, husband, brother, and good person."

Uncle Earnest: "As a person who gave his all. He was a person who looked out for his fellow man. He respected all. He didn't take advantage of others because of his intellect. He gave back and was always helpful. He was a sharing and caring person."

Gerald Mackie: "A fighter for the cause."

Uncle Joe: "He was very involved." Uncle Joe shared that my father was very active in the Orangeburg County meeting with elected officials that met monthly. Orangeburg County at that time was ~80% African American. He also shared that my father encouraged former Congressman John Matthews of Orangeburg to run for that position.

Yes, I believe it is such a disservice to our loved ones when we don't honor their memories after they die as I stated earlier in the book. We want to honor the dead to show our love and remember the joy, sorrows, and fun we had with them.

*My favorite picture with my father.*

# Chapter 14 - My Growth and Healing in Unexpected Ways

**My Growth through this Process**

*"Person who worked hard, wanted to see change in the world, he really wanted to see change in the world." Aunt Earline McClary*

This is how she felt my father would want to be remembered.

Writing this book about my father helped me better understand members of my family who were impacted by his death, and I got to know my mother better, his friends, and myself. This was an unexpected additional learning that I didn't expect since everyone I talked to knew my father at different times and had their own vantage points. It was great to see such similarities of who he was as a brilliant, kind, and loving person.

As I wrote this book to collect memories of my father, I have been blessed beyond measure. I have grown emotionally and mentally. I gained additional strength and awareness of my power and strengthened my connection with my father, which I felt ended when he died. I felt robbed of the opportunity to know him, though he was never able to see me again on this earth after his death- I am thankful to be able to meet him again on this side through memories shared by family and friends. I look forward to seeing him in heaven when that time comes.

I learned more about myself, our common areas of strengths, and more similarities between my children and my father. My youngest son physically resembles my father and has a similar body frame and complexion. Both of my sons are extremely intelligent, like my father. I called my youngest son "professor", when he was younger, since he liked to share facts with us, and when talking with Aunt Lula, she shared that some called my father "Mr. Professor" at their church. I was shocked to hear this reference. I learned from talking with my cousin Adam that my father liked Rock music and introduced him to Jimi Hendrix. My oldest son also likes Rock music and many other forms of music. I am not a big Rock fan, but love many forms of music.

I shared with many of the people I interviewed that memories could return to them after we spoke and offered that if they wanted to share more with me after this initial discussion, that would be fine. I didn't expect during this process that more of my own memories of my childhood would resurface during this process. It was a good experience. With each interview, more dots were connected for me about my father and his life, the love shared by the family and friends for him, and the love he shared for his family and friends. I was surprised by how, towards the end of writing this book, more memories of growing up returned to me. For example, I remembered more about my grandparents and the trips we would take to visit other relatives in the area. It was a peaceful time for me as these memories came back. Some thoughts returned that I had not thought about for a long time, so that was very surprising to me. I am more confident and complete and thankful to have gaps closed about my father and my heritage through this process.

*A treasured picture with my Mom.*

A Bible verse states, "But you are a chosen people, a royal priesthood, a holy nation, God's special possession, that you may declare the praises of him who called you out of darkness into his wonderful light." 1 Peter 2:9 NIV

Being able to better understand my father and my lineage helps me better appreciate and understand the richness of my father, my genetics, the legacy of my father, and my personal legacy, gifts, greatness, and the impact I can have in the world and my family for future generations. I am proud of the person my father was and honored to live out this life with a better & more complete understanding of him and continue to acknowledge his legacy through my life and my children. I hope that by sharing his life with others, the love and memories we all shared with him will last forever and encourage others to support his legacy and the legacy of other loved ones who have died. Allowing their memories to be shared and lives honored through future generations.

I hope that the pain of loss will be healed and that we allow ourselves time and space to grieve and rejoice as we treasure the love shared and memories made. We have a hope that we will meet our loved ones again in heaven, but until that time, we can still honor them through sharing their memories, recalling their lives, and speaking their names with others in the family, world, and community.

## Some bonds remain- regardless of time, pain, loss, or death

I am stronger and happier as a result of going through this tremendous journey to capture memories of my father and come to know him further. I am thankful to know these facts about him after the age of 18 months when he died. I am happy to share his memory and life with my children, husband, family members, and the world. I am thankful to be his daughter, whom he named. I am honored to be a part of a loving and powerful legacy that will remain.

My heart is overjoyed with love and compassion for all those who took time to go back over forty – five years to share memories with me. You have blessed me and my family more than you can ever know or imagine. This woman who lost her father tragically before I was two years old, who only shared one birthday party with him and 18 months together, now has the rest of my life to enjoy the memories you shared with me of his life, impact, and journey. You have allowed me to reconnect with him and share his legacy with others, especially my children. You have allowed me to share his life as the gem and treasure it was. You helped me give him another hug and allowed us to smile at each other again. It is a gift I am eternally grateful for. I urge others to share stories of loved ones' past with their children, family, and friends to help them grow, heal, and thrive!

I believe we all can have a chance to heal and embrace our loved ones' memories and legacy to become whole and lean into and fully embrace what God has designed each of us to provide to the world and others. Sometimes we may even be called to continue or share the great work and lives our loved ones had so that others can know them and continue their legacy and impact.

# Chapter 15 - A Life Well Lived, Gratitude and Legacy

**Love Never Dies**

To my father, William Lee Holman,

You have returned to me in spirit, and I am thankful to learn about your childhood, teenage years, and adult years. I am so happy to learn about your challenges, dreams, achievements, gifts, brilliance, and goals you had in life. I am thankful to see the love you shared with my mom and me, family, friends, for Black people and all people. I am thankful for the work and efforts you supported and led to improve the lives of Black people in the 1960s and 1970s until your unexpected tragic death in 1977. I recognize and honor your commitment to activism and equal rights. I will continue to share your memory and legacy with others and thank you for the love and time you gave me and for being my father. Thank you for your life and impact. I have always been proud to be a Holman, and on this day, as this book draws to an end, it grows even more as I learn more about who you were and your light, power, love, and brilliance. Thank you for being you and sharing your life and gifts with us.

God,

Thank you for instructing me to write this book on my father. You instructed me to write this book in 2022, and I am honored to share this work with the world. Thank you for choosing me to share my father's story and life with others. Thank you for allowing me to heal, grow, and get stronger. Thank you for the opportunity to share his journey and my family and his friends' journey with others.

As I close this chapter of honoring my father's life with this book I have established another lasting way to support causes he embraced - education and community advancement. As an additional way to support my father's legacy, the William Lee Holman Legacy Education & Community Foundation was formed in Oct 2023.

We are a non-profit, charitable 501c3 organization focused on supporting students in South Carolina with scholarships to promote educational enrichment and advancement following high school graduation for individuals and under-served communities. We will support additional community and educational efforts for economic growth, financial literacy, and equality in education. To learn more about our foundation or to contribute to our foundation , please visit https://williamleeholmanfoundation.org and contact us at info@williamleeholmanfoundation.org. We are honored to continue my father's life, love, and legacy!

*My father, William Lee Holman forever in our hearts.*

# Afterword

Life has a way of coming full circle at times to provide clarity, closure and direction simultaneously. My journey to capture and share memories of my father has provided all three of these for me. It has been a journey that changed my life, the lives of my children and future generations. It has allowed me to continue my father's legacy with a better understanding of him, his work, love, vision and impact.

I am eternally grateful for the opportunity to take this journey during my lifetime and be able to share these memories with my children and the world. My hope is that they will continue the legacy of their grandfather , continue to stay close to our extended family and make a positive impact on the world through their lives.

I encourage anyone else dealing with grief, loss, or questions regarding their loved ones to seek the answers they desire to restore their spirits and deepen their family connections and legacy and in particular for families and children impacted by loss.

I especially want to thank my husband, Dexter, and our children, Christian and Nathan who encouraged me and saw me on my good days and my challenging moments as I worked to complete this book. Special thanks to everyone I interviewed for sharing your memories with me. Thank you to my friends, immediate, and extended family for your unwavering support during this time. My Mom holds a more dear place in my heart for her strength, love & wisdom. Thank you for helping me through this process.

Thank you to my book editors, Maurice Gray, Jr and Andrea Price. You were a dynamic duo of support. Andrea, thank you for being a great Writing Coach for my first book. Fred Nash thank you for graphic design support and providing a wonderful book cover that captures the essence of my father. I will continue to honor my father's legacy and continue to live my life in a way that makes a difference in the world as I fulfill my destiny.

# About the Author

Kaisha McCrea is a certified Career & Leadership Coach and CEO & Founder of Growing Perspectives Career Consulting. She has always loved writing and journalism from her youth and is honored to share stories with the world through writing. She resides in Virginia with her husband, Dexter and their two sons, Nathan and Christian. She enjoys public speaking to empower others for career and leadership growth. She is a recognized leader in her community and recognized as a Top 15 Coach in Richmond, VA for 2023 by Influence Digest + and as the 2022 Member of the Year by Chesterfield Chamber of Commerce in Virginia. She has held several leadership roles within her career and in the community including serving on Board of Directors. She is also the President of the William Lee Holman Legacy Education & Community Foundation.

She is active in her local church and has a strong anchor in her Christian faith and love for God, family and friends. She is a continuous learner and committed to fulfilling the mission God has designed for her life. She previously worked in Corporate America for over 20 years in various roles starting as an Engineer after college. She has a desire to support people and organizations to grow & thrive in their careers & lives. She is excited to live her life to the fullest and make a difference in the world. She can be contacted at KaishaMcCrea@gmail.com.